Advances in Developing Human Resources

Number 5, 2000

Richard A. Swanson

Editor-in-Chief

Strategic Perspectives on Knowledge, Competence, and Expertise

Richard W. Herling & Joanne Provo, Editors

AHRD

THE ACADEMY OF HUMAN RESOURCE DEVELOPMENT

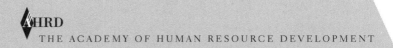

BK

BERRETT–KOEHLER COMMUNICATIONS, INC.

Advances in Developing Human Resources (ISSN 1523-4223) is a quarterly monograph series published by the Academy of Human Resource Development and Berrett-Koehler Communications, Inc.

Academy of Human Resource Development
P.O. Box 25113
Baton Rouge, LA 70894-5113

Berrett-Koehler Communications, Inc.
450 Sansome Street, Suite 1200
San Francisco, CA 94111-4825

Subscription Orders: Please send subscription orders to Berrett-Koehler Communications, PO Box 565, Williston, VT 05495, or call 800-929-2929, or fax 802-864-7626. Subscriptions cost $79 for individuals and $125 for institutions. All orders must be prepaid in U.S. dollars or charged to Visa, MasterCard, or American Express. For orders outside the United States, please add $15 for surface mail or $30 for air mail. Librarians are encouraged to write for a free sample issue.

Editorial Correspondence: Address editorial correspondence and inquiries to Richard A. Swanson, Editor-in-Chief, *Advances in Developing Human Resources*, University of Minnesota, 1954 Buford Avenue, Suite 425, St. Paul, MN 55108, USA. E-mail: swanson2@cris.com

Library of Congress Cataloging-in-Publication Data

Strategic perspectives on knowledge, competence, & expertise / Richard W. Herling & Joanne Provo, editors.
p. cm. — (Advances in developing human resources)
A collection of 7 chapters written by the editors and other authors.
Includes bibliographical references and index.
ISBN 1-58376-057-1
1. Knowledge management. 2. Organizational learning.. 3. Employees—Training of. 4. Human capital I. Herling, Richard W. II. Provo, Joanne. III. Series.
HD30.2 .S7895 2000
658.4'038–dc21   00-021888

 Printed in the United States of America on acid-free and recycled paper.

Postmaster: Please send address changes to the Berrett-Koehler address above.
Cover Design: Carolyn Deacy Design, San Francisco, CA
Production: Pleasant Run Publishing Services, Williamsburg, VA

Contents

Gioia and Sims (1986) begin *The Thinking Organization* with this statement: "People in organizations are not simply 'actors.' They are unique in that they do not just *do,* they also *think.* More accurately, perhaps, they often take action as a result of their thinking" (p. 1).

Thinking people who take action: this is what the seven contributing authors of this book envision as the essence of human capital. Although people have always been recognized as an integral part of the organization, only recently has the workforce itself been viewed as a valuable asset. Now organizations must engage in the process of bringing into play the strategic potential that lies in the combined knowledge, competence, and expertise of its workforce.

Overview of the Book

This book represents a mere dipping of toes into the ocean that metaphorically represents the little that is known and the much that is unknown about organizational knowledge, competence, and expertise. It provides a glimpse into a much larger world that is waiting to be explored—a world where organizational strategy represents a process focused on the creation and flow of valuable information, developing the core competencies that make the organization unique, and keeping the entire organization expertise rich.

The book starts by looking at human capital from a theoretical perspective and finishes from a perspective of application. The first and second chapters support the development of a foundational understanding of the elements of human capital management. Chapter 1 examines the roles and relationships that knowledge, competence, and expertise take on when human capital management is seen as part of an organization's strategic positioning. Chapter 2 specifically looks at the nature and characteristics of human expertise.

The third and fourth chapters examine the two theoretical components of intellectual capital and knowledge management. The existing theories and concepts of intellectual capital are presented in Chapter 3, which focuses on the dynamic impact that intellectual capital can have on the organization. Springboarding off this, Chapter 4 begins with the premise that knowledge is a complex and intangible asset with unique cultural and technical dimensions. It then draws on existing theory and recent empirical studies to develop a theory of knowledge management.

The fifth and sixth chapters discuss applications of human capital management theory from two different perspectives. Chapter 5 takes the training and development perspective in demonstrating how the economic theories of gaming and human capital provide a conceptual model for forecasting the strategic potential of a training initiative. Chapter 6, presenting an organization development perspective, highlights the shortcomings of financial-based techniques for assessing the value of human capital and outlines a new, strategic approach to human resource measurement.

The seventh and final chapter pulls all the concepts together as it examines organizational knowledge, competence, and expertise from the context of strategic planning and discusses some of the implications this holds for the organization.

Acknowledgments

We thank all those individuals who supported this effort through their reviews, suggestions, recommendations, and encouragement.

Richard W. Herling
Joanne Provo

Reference

Sims, H. P., Gioia, D. A., & Associates. (1986). *The thinking organization: Dynamics of organizational social cognition.* San Francisco: Jossey-Bass.

Chapter 1

▲ Knowledge, Competence, and Expertise in Organizations

Richard W. Herling
Joanne Provo

The Problem and the Solution. Many organizations fail to recognize that the management of an organization's human capital is about keeping the entire organization talent rich, focusing on developing the core competencies that make the organization unique, and managing the creation and flow of valuable information. This chapter examines the roles and strategic perspectives of knowledge, competence, and expertise, key concepts to managing the organization's human capital effectively.

It has become difficult to pick up a business-oriented journal or book that has not made some reference to knowledge, or the management of knowledge, as being the new competitive tool of organizations (and clearly this book is not going to be an exception). *Knowledge assets, intellectual capital, human capital, core competencies, organizational expertise,* and *the learning organization,* each representing legitimate and fundamentally sound concepts, have risen to the top as the new buzzwords of progressive management. Numerous authors (Senge, 1990; Quinn, 1992; Pfeffer, 1994, 1998; Swanson, 1994) have stressed the importance of recognizing the organization's human resources, particularly the knowledge, capabilities, and expertise possessed by the organization's employees, as being not only a significant competitive advantage but also, and more important, a sustainable one. Yet these capital assets are not a competitive advantage unless, or until, the organization adopts a strategic perspective of knowledge, competence, and expertise.

The concept of having and using a strategy originated, and remains firmly rooted, in the practice of warfare. A strategy has always represented a plan, or intended series of actions, to be used for gaining advantage over one's enemies; therefore, to be successful, a strategy had to remain undetected by the enemy until it was too late to counter it effectively. Today, even in the larger contextual world of work, there are some organizations that have retained this historical perspective, developing complex and highly secret plans as they wage their constant battle for market share. However, for most organizations, a strategy merely represents a plan for achieving goals and moving forward. These strategic plans are generally focused on how best to leverage one's assets, and the organization's human resources are now being recognized as a very important asset.

Regardless of which term is used (*people, workforce, human resources, human capital,* or *human assets*) the expertise and the capacity to do work that groups of individuals bring every day to the organizations they serve clearly have value. It is just as clear to see that the management, or mismanagement, of this human element directly affects an organization's ability to achieve its goals and move forward. This human-based asset is primarily composed of the knowledge, capabilities, and expertise that the organization's employees possess.

Having a plan to manage the organization's human capital is critical. To develop that plan, an organization requires a strategic perspective related to knowledge, competence, and expertise.

Viewing Knowledge from a Strategic Perspective

Many believe that the accessibility of knowledge is the foundation for establishing a competitive advantage (Edvinsson & Malone, 1997; Torraco & Swanson, 1995). Knowledge is the base-level component of human capital and without question an organizational asset. However, it is a complex and intangible asset, and because of the cultural and technical dimensions of knowledge, Torraco (see Chapter 4) argues that it cannot be managed like other resources.

At a fundamental level, the management of knowledge must address its acquisition, creation, storage, redistribution, and application. Most important, it must be constantly assessed for the value it has to the organization. Stewart (1997) argues that to be of value, knowledge must be specifically described, shared, exploited, and deployed within the organization to do something that could not be done if the knowledge remained unmanaged. If knowledge is acquired or created with no application to the organization's business operations, then it cannot be employed in the creation of value for the organization. Knowledge that has no value is reduced to mere information, and Stewart (1997) makes it clear that knowledge assets, like money or capital assets, exist and are worth developing only in the context of organizational strategy.

Recognizing knowledge as an asset is only one strategic perspective of knowledge. Organizations must also recognize the unique characteristics and value of knowledge work and knowledge workers. The rise of knowledge work and knowledge workers has created demands for new types of training and development in such areas as knowledge transformation, competency building, continuous technology training, and knowledge awareness training. When viewed from the overall context of human capital, the strategic perspective of knowledge has to consider not only how knowledge is created and applied, but also how it is leveraged for value. This strategic perspective of knowledge is key to the management of human capital.

Viewing Competence from a Strategic Perspective

Sveiby (1997) expands the definition of human capital to include the concept of employee competence, or the capacity of employees to act in a wide variety of situations. *Competence*, a term frequently used but not clearly understood, implies an ability to demonstrate a consistent level of performance. Individual competency is commonly defined as a cluster of related factual knowledge, skills, experiences, attitudes, and value judgments directly related to one's job (Parry, 1998). From this perspective, it is generally assumed that individual or employee competence correlates with performance on the job, that it can be measured against well-accepted standards, and that it can be improved with training and practice.

The problem with competence, at least when the organization chooses to place its emphasis on individual competence, is that it is limiting. Although all organizations expect and desire to have high-performing employees, the reality is that the standards of being competent can only be equated with a minimum acceptable level of performance. A more strategic perspective for organizations is to link human capital management and knowledge management to the creation of sustainable core competencies (Prahalad & Hamel, 1990).

Core competencies refer to the particular business expertise that an organization has developed. The core competence of the organization is a unique combination of business specialization and human skills that gives expression to its typical character (Bergenhenegouwen, ten Horn, & Mooijman, 1996)—for example, the ability to get unbiased information.

Whereas skills tend to be specific and situational, competencies are generic and universal. A core competence is characterized by three traits: it makes a contribution to perceived customer benefits, it is difficult for competitors to imitate, and it can be leveraged to a wide variety of markets (Prahalad & Hamel, 1990). Core competencies are difficult for competitors to duplicate because they are distinctive and specific to each individual organization. Concentrating on the core competencies makes the organization highly effective.

From a strategic perspective, the real potential of an organization is expressed in its core competencies. Business success increasingly is based on the improvement and strengthening of the core business of the individual organization. When viewed from the overall context of the management of human capital, a strategic perspective of competence, like knowledge, has multiple facets. At the individual level, the organization's strategic perspective must consider the desired general competencies to be used in the selection and development decisions of its workforce. More important, from a strategic perspective, the organization must focus on the development and growth of its own core competencies.

Viewing Expertise from a Strategic Perspective

Core competencies are defined by focusing on the organization's critical success factors and values and on the particular challenges it expects to face over the next five years and beyond. For example, young organizations need leaders to help them manage their growth; expanding, mid-sized companies need executives to explore new opportunities while maintaining profitability; and mature companies need leaders to help reinvent themselves. Within the context of work, what is generally accepted from the employee is a minimum level of performance despite the fact that what is desired, and often required, from the organization's workforce is outstanding performance.

Outstanding performance is a displayed characteristic of expertise. Individual expertise, not unlike competence, comprises related value judgments, knowledge and skill sets, lived experiences, and problem-solving abilities. However, unlike competence, which tends to be generic and universal, expertise is domain specific and therefore unique. The core competencies of an organization are built on the expertise of its workforce. The example of leadership as a core competency embodies the important, and related, concept of acquired individual expertise. Continuing with this example, organizations that have leadership as a core competency have strong, effective leaders at every level, from assistant supervisor up through the ranks of the executive officers. Each individual in each leadership role has developed and demonstrated the expertise associated with being an outstanding performer at his or her respective level. Despite the fact that each leadership role is unique and can be associated with a different set of accountabilities and requirements, the requirements of leadership at the organizational level can only be defined in broad universal terms as a competency.

When considering expertise from a strategic perspective, the development of domain-specific skills and knowledge is a critical factor. Expertise has a second characteristic that makes it unique: it takes years to develop. Research has shown that individual expertise is developed through extensive and intensive training and practice (Ericsson & Charness, 1994), requiring an individual to acquire an estimated minimum of ten thousand hours of related domain-specific training and experience before achieving recognition as an expert (Bereiter & Scardamalia, 1993).

Swanson (1994), in stressing the importance of expertise to the organization, metaphorically describes individual expertise as being the performance fuel of the workplace. Because expertise is domain specific, it is not readily transferable, and the long learning curve associated with its development makes it difficult for an organization to acquire core competencies readily (Boyett, 1995).

Having a competent workforce allows the organization to maintain its competitive position. To move the organization forward and grow requires highly knowledgeable and skilled individuals capable of solving progressively more difficult and unique situational problems. In short, sustained organizational success requires employee expertise, not employee competence.

Conclusion

Long-term organizational success is linked to the organization's ability to develop and leverage its human capital—the knowledge, capabilities, and expertise of its employees. Strategies associated with the management of human capital must consider how most effectively to develop core competencies through on-the-job experiences, how to provide employees with training programs designed to develop the specific knowledge and expertise required for these targeted competencies, how to promote self-insight and encourage self-management of the development process, and how to create and disseminate new knowledge.

These are not easy tasks. Harris (see Chapter 3) discusses the issues associated with leveraging explicit knowledge and implicit knowledge, the latter being the critical knowledge that experienced individuals possess but are not readily identified or transferred within the organization, and Krohn (see Chapter 5) identifies some of the concerns associated with investing in the development of employee expertise.

The management of an organization's human capital is about keeping the entire organization talent rich, focusing on developing knowledge and experience within the core competencies and managing the creation and flow of valuable information. In short, it is about the strategic perspectives that organizations take regarding knowledge, competence, and expertise—the work of human resource development and of organizational leaders. The following chapters present thoughtful analyses of these core ideas, ideas that deserve study and reflection prior to taking action and implementing programs.

References

Bereiter, C., & Scardamalia, M. (1993). *Surpassing ourselves: An inquiry into the nature and implications of expertise.* Chicago: Open Court.

Bergenhenegouwen, G. J., ten Horn, H. F. K., & Mooijman, E. A. M. (1996, September). Competence development—a challenge for HRM professionals: Core competencies of organizations as guidelines for the development of employees. *Journal of European Industrial Training, 20,* 29–35.

Boyett, J. H. (1995). *Beyond workplace 2000: Essential strategies for the new American corporation.* New York: Penguin Books.

Edvinsson, L., & Malone, M. (1997). *Intellectual capital: Realizing your company's true value by finding its hidden brainpower.* New York: Harper Business.

Ericsson, K. A., & Charness, N. (1994). Expert performance: Its structure and acquisition. *American Psychologist, 49,* 725–747.

Parry, S. B. (1998, June). Just what is a competency? (And why should you care?) *Training, 35,* 58–62.

Pfeffer, J. (1994). *Competitive advantage through people: Unleashing the power of the work force.* Boston: Harvard Business School Press.

Pfeffer, J. (1998). *The human equation: Building profits by putting people first.* Boston: Harvard Business School Press.

Prahalad, C. K., & Hamel, G. (1990). The core competence of the corporation. *Harvard Business Review, 68*(3), 79–91.

Quinn, J. B. (1992). *Intelligent enterprise.* New York: Free Press.

Senge, P. (1990). *The fifth discipline: The art and practice of the learning organization.* New York: Doubleday.

Stewart, T. A. (1997). *Intellectual capital: The new wealth of organizations.* New York: Doubleday/Currency.

Sveiby, K. E. (1997). *The new organizational wealth: Managing & measuring knowledge-based assets.* San Francisco: Berrett-Koehler.

Swanson, R. A. (1994). *Analysis for improving performance: Tools for diagnosing organizations and documenting workplace expertise.* San Francisco: Berrett-Koehler.

Torraco, R. J., & Swanson, R. A. (1995). The strategic roles of human resource development. *Human Resource Planning, 18*(4), 10–21.

▲ Operational Definitions of Expertise and Competence

Richard W. Herling

The Problem and the Solution. The concept of human expertise is fundamental to the human resource practices. Although exemplary performance can
be clearly recognized in the actions of others, organizations lack a means of
measuring expertise. The need to quantify expertise is critical to being able to
manage and develop the organization's human capital effectively. This chapter
examines the basic characteristics of expertise and develops an operational
definition of human expertise.

After a decade of downsizing, right sizing, restructuring, reor-
ganizing, and reengineering (various perceived methods of
attaining profitability), organizations are beginning to realize that their
workforce, the operating expense most easily reduced, is also their resource
with the biggest impact on attaining and maintaining long-term profitability and growth. An organization's human resources are now being
recognized as a significant competitive advantage and one of the hidden
forces behind growth, profits, and lasting value (Pfeffer, 1994; Reichheld,
1996). As Torraco and Swanson (1995) noted, "Business success increasingly hinges on an organization's ability to use its employees' expertise as
a factor in the shaping of its business strategy" (p. 11). It is the skills, knowledge, and experience of the organization's human resources—in short, its
expertise—that must be recognized as the organization's most important
competitive advantage.

Clearly, human expertise is of primary interest to organizations; it is
also of unquestionable importance to the management of human capital.
A conceptual understanding of expertise, as it specifically applies to indi-

vidual performance, is a basic requirement for managing human capital, and fundamental to this conceptual understanding is the need for operational definitions of expertise and competence.

Rationale for an Operational Definition of Expertise

McLagan (1997) has noted that organizations are beginning to realize how their market value increasingly relies on the knowledge and skills of their employees and that caring about their (human) competency base and how it is developed is starting to make strategic sense to them.

Jacobs (1997) has defined employee competence as the potential to use specific sets of knowledge and skills, noting that it "should be viewed within its proper performance context" (p. 281), and McLagan (1997) has stated that a competent workforce is well within the grasp of any organization. Nevertheless, in today's competitive business environment, just being competent is not enough.

The term *competence* suggests that an employee has an ability to do something satisfactory—not necessarily outstandingly or even well, but rather to a minimum level of acceptable performance. Today, rapid change within the organization is inevitable, and the organization's performance context is being constantly redefined. What is required for adapting to change is not just competent individuals but individuals who are outstanding performers. As represented by Swanson's taxonomy of performance (1994, p. 57), the skills and knowledge required to maintain a system are significantly different from the *expertise* required to change and improve the organization and its systems. To gain competitive advantage and be adaptive to change, organizations are requiring that employees be top performers. Thus, it is the development of workplace expertise, not merely competence, that is becoming vital to optimal organization performance.

In the context of individual performance and human resource development, expertise is defined as "the optimal level at which a person is able and/or expected to perform within a specialized realm of human activity" (Swanson, 1994, p. 94). As a descriptive definition of human expertise, this provides clarity and focus, and expertise is generally thought of as the possession of superior skills or knowledge in a particular area of study. Expertise is also generally recognized as implying proficiency, with an understanding that an individual gains expertise, and thus proficiency, only through experience and training.

The importance of quantifying expertise has long been recognized. Although an individual's general level of expertise is readily observable through his or her actions, this ease of recognition has tended to promote what can be interpreted as a misdirected attempt to quantify human expertise: the classification and reclassification of individual levels of expertise. From the traditional terminology of the craft guilds of the Middle Ages to Jacobs's (1997) proposed taxonomy of expertise for human resource development (HRD), a myriad of terms, ranging from *novice* to *expert*, have been used to describe and define human expertise and varying levels of expertness (Jacobs, 1997; Hoffman, Shadbolt, Burton, & Klein, 1995; Bereiter & Scardamalia, 1993). Unfortunately, the actual measurement of expertise has never been fully defined, and the classification of human expertise without the ability to measure expertise quantitatively has limited utility.

It is generally accepted that the primary tool for linking individual performance to that of the organization, for the purpose of taking improvement action, is measurement. In fact, Rummler and Brache (1995) noted that it is only through measurement that performance can be monitored, managed, and improved. Swanson (1994) more directly states that "it is foolhardy to talk about development, change, and performance improvement without specifying the measure of performance" (p. 53).

Thus, logic seems to dictate that the quantification and measurement of expertise are necessary if an organization is to be able to improve its performance and the performance of its human resources.

Theoretical Perspectives of Expertise

In the past thirty years, entire books, complete chapters, and a multitude of papers have been written in response to the question, What is expertise? (Chi, Glaser, & Farr, 1988; Slatter, 1990; Ericcson & Smith, 1991; Bereiter & Scardamalia, 1993; Swanson, 1994; Kuchinke, 1997), and the answers have been numerous and varied. However, it does not require an in-depth review of the literature to develop a basic conceptual understanding of expertise. The nature of expertise can be easily gleaned from a brief examination of two major theoretical perspectives.

Overview of the Cognitive Theories of Expertise

From a psychological perspective, all research on experts and expertise began with the study of chess players by deGoot and the publication of his findings in 1965 (Kuchinke, 1997). The research activity that immediately followed this event focused on the comparative differences in performance between experts and nonexperts.

This initial exploration of the individual's basic information-processing and problem-solving capabilities led to a second generation of research that focused on the expert's abilities to solve complex problems. The resulting theories saw the identification of expert characteristics as being the key to understanding human expertise. The outcome of this refocused research effort, as summarized by Glaser and Chi (1988) and included in Kuchinke's (1997) update of the current theories and literature, was the identification of several key characteristics associated with either how experts solve problems or how experts acquire, process, and retrieve information. Briefly summarized, experts know more, use the information they have differently, and solve problems faster.

Research on expertise theory is still evolving. Based on a realization that there may be no single expert way, current theory and research work are examining expertise as the "ability to rapidly organize and process small bits of information into meaningful and creative solutions to specific problems" (Kuchinke, 1997).

Overview of the Knowledge Engineering Theories of Expertise

While the cognitive psychologists attempted to discover what was required to be an expert, knowledge engineering, another area of study highly interested in human expertise, took a different approach and focused on the replication of human expertise.

Through their attempts to create artificial intelligence, knowledge engineers focused on how an expert thinks. The results and findings of their research closely paralleled that of the cognitive psychologists. The knowledge engineers theorized and modeled expertise as a thinking process, and over the decades have formulated five major model classifications of human expertise: heuristic models, deep models, implicit models, competence models, and distributed models (Slatter, 1990).

In the beginning, the heuristic models loosely defined expertise as the acquisition of lots of information, including heuristic knowledge—knowledge about a specific domain. The organization of this knowledge—the hierarchical relationships, causal models, and schemata representations of domain knowledge that supported advanced problem solving—was explained by the deep models. The implicit models that followed this initial work attempted to explain expertise by differentiating between implicit knowledge and explicit knowledge. In this context, explicit knowledge was seen to encompass the known facts of a specific domain, while implicit knowledge represented the "non-articulable experience-base knowledge that enables a skilled expert to solve a task in an effortless, seemingly intuitive fashion" (Slatter, 1990, p. 141).

The competence models made a distinction between domain knowledge (static knowledge) and task knowledge (action knowledge). The implication was that *expertise* is a competence-level term denoting the potential for *doing something*. These models of expertise recognize that experts know a great deal about a specific domain and that experts use this knowledge to solve problems. Task knowledge, which is gained from the practice of domain-specific behaviors, is compiled by the expert within his or her domain of knowledge in an ongoing search for better ways to do things, including problem solving. The underlying assumption of the distributed models is that the expertise to solve complex problems may be distributed among many individuals. Thus distributed models equate expertise as a combination of domain knowledge, task knowledge, and cooperative knowledge.

Elements of Expertise

Although a large body of knowledge has been, and continues to be, added to our understanding of the nature of expertise, after thirty years of advancing research on this topic, neither the cognitive psychologists nor the knowledge engineers have been able to agree on exactly what expertise is. In fact, Kuchinke's (1997) review of the expertise theories and Slatter's (1990) summary explanation of the knowledge engineers' expertise models have shown, through a lack of consensus, that human expertise cannot be operationally defined by its processes. However, the combined summaries of these two reviewers have brought to the light several commonly shared elements in the various theories of expertise:

(1) expertise is a dynamic state, (2) expertise is domain specific, and (3) the basic components of expertise can be identified as knowledge, experience, and problem solving. Figure 2.1 is a representation of the relationship of these three foundational concepts of expertise.

From this perspective, the most important concept of human expertise is that it is a dynamic state; an internal process of continuous learning is characterized by the constant acquisition of knowledge, reorganization of information, and progressive solving of problems. Bereiter and Scardamalia (1993) summarized this dynamic characteristic of expertise in their descriptive comparison of experts and nonexperts: "[The] career of the expert is one of progressively advancing on problems constituting a field of work, whereas the career of the non-expert is one of gradually constricting the field of work so that it more closely conforms to the routines the non-expert is prepared to execute" (p. 11).

Equally important is the fact that expertise is recognized as domain specific. The majority of research suggests that extensive, specialized knowledge is "required for excellence in most fields" (Gleespen, 1996, p. 502). Research also indicates that "there is little evidence that a person highly skilled in one domain can transfer the skill to another" (Glaser & Chi, 1988, p. xvii). Cognitive psychologists have theorized that "there are some domains where nearly everyone becomes an expert, like reading English words" (Posner,

▲ **Figure 2.1   Basic Components of Expertise**

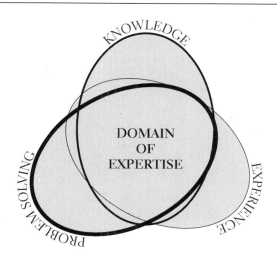

1988, p. xxxi), but note that the demonstration of expertise in one domain is no guarantee of expertise in other areas (Glaser, 1985, p. 7).

The third foundational concept is that expertise has a few basic components. Although there was not always agreement among the researchers as to which component took precedence, all identified in some manner knowledge, experience, and problem solving as the distinguishing points of difference between experts and nonexperts. These three common elements can be viewed as the fundamental components of human expertise. Each is clearly measurable, and it is reasonable to expect that an operational definition of expertise can be developed from them.

The Component of Knowledge

Knowledge appeared in every reviewed theory and model of expertise, and in almost every case it was either descriptively different or multiple types of knowledge were specified.

Depending on the theories or models being examined, the knowledge required for expertise could be implicit or explicit, shallow or deep, task specific or heuristic. Bereiter and Scardamalia (1993), in their inquiry into the nature of expertise, noted that "every kind of knowledge has a part in expertise" (p. 74). Their definition for every kind of knowledge included what they classified as the obvious kinds of knowledge — procedural knowledge and formal knowledge — as well as what they referred to as the less obvious kinds: informal knowledge, impressionistic knowledge, and self-regulatory knowledge.

Although there may be some disagreement among the theories and models regarding the specific type of knowledge required for expertise, the theorists are in agreement on two points. First, for the purposes of expertise, knowledge is, and has to be, domain specific. Second, knowledge is an interactive component of expertise; it is one of the requirements for expertise but is not expertise in itself. As Bereiter and Scardamalia (1993) noted, nonexperts as well as experts have knowledge; "the difference," they say, "is in how much they have, how well integrated it is, and how effectively it is geared to performance" (p. 74).

The Component of Experience

Just as it is recognized that all experts are knowledgeable, it is also understood from the theories that all experts are experienced. Based on their studies of master's-level chess players, Chase and Simon (1973, cited by Posner, 1988) "reasoned that to achieve a master level of expertise a player had to spend between 10,000 and 20,000 hours staring at chess positions" (p. xxxi). A number of years later, through the studied biographies of experts in many fields, it was generalized that ten thousand hours was the minimum amount of time required to gain expert experience (Bereiter & Scardamalia, 1993, p. 17). Thus, it has been hypothesized from research that to become an expert, one must have the equivalent of ten years of combined studies and related work experience.

Unfortunately, *experience*, not unlike *expertise*, is a term of varied meanings and currently lacking qualifying and quantifying boundaries. Experience, an interactive component of expertise, is heavily dependent on the type, quality, and quantity of the events that the individual experiences. As Bereiter and Scardamalia (1993) observed in the performance of equally experienced school teachers (based on the training received and the number of years worked), experience "distinguishes old-timers from beginners, but does not distinguish experts from experienced non-experts" (p. 81).

The Component of Problem Solving

The key to expertise thus appears to lie in an individual's propensity to solve problems. The knowledge engineers, in attempting to replicate the process of applying expertise, have viewed problem solving as the core concept of expertise, and like the concept of knowledge, they have ended up describing and identifying a multitude of problem-solving processes.

The concept of problem solving as the primary component of expertise has also been heavily supported by the research of cognitive psychologists (Glaser, 1987, cited by Chi et al., 1988). Problem solving, as the term is currently used in cognitive psychology, constitutes some amount of searching or deliberation in order to find a way to achieve a goal, a concept that defines a problem as any nonroutine purposeful activity (Bereiter & Scardamalia, 1993).

Max Wertheimer, an early gestalt psychologist whose studies and research centered on insightful learning, believed that problem solutions depended on the previous experience of the problem solver, noting that "the prime difference was in the originality used by the problem-solver to organize information" (Hill, 1971, p. 102). This concept of experience as leading to insightful solutions is also reflected in Bereiter and Scardamalia's

(1993) description of expert and nonexpert problem-solving activity. Bereiter and Scardamalia see problem solving as the single dynamic element in the growth of expertise and experts as being progressive problem solvers, while "the problem-solving efforts of the non-expert are taken over by well learned routines…aimed at eliminating still more problems thus reducing the activity even further" (p. 81).

An Operational Definition of Human Expertise

This examination of the foundational components of expertise shows that nonexperts can have vast amounts of knowledge, can have many years of experience, and can also solve problems. Thus, an operational definition of expertise based on the combined elements would appear to have little value.

It is generally agreed that the presence of expertise is readily recognized in an individual's actions. The remaining option is to work from the premise that we know expertise when we see it. Basing an operational definition on the characteristics of displayed behavior carries with it a degree of practicality.

Experts are capable of doing things at a higher level; they have more knowledge, a greater skill level, and better solutions than nonexperts do (VanLehn, 1989). The expert-novice research of different occupations (domains) has verified that this is true (Glaser & Chi, 1988; VanLehn, 1989; Ericcson & Smith, 1991). The fundamental basis of expert research has been driven by the recognized fact that there were observed differences in the displayed behavior of individuals engaged in the same activities. Thus, it is reasonable to assume that the concept of "demonstrated behavior" can be used as the foundational core of an operational definition of human expertise.

Behavior, as applied to the discussion of human expertise, implies an intended action on the part of the individual. An action has a consequence; it terminates with a result. Results, and the actions that lead to them, are measurable. Gilbert (1996), equating individual performance to a transactional relationship involving both a behavior and its consequence, believed that the result of behavior should be viewed in the context of value—"the consequence as a valuable accomplishment" or "valuable performance" (p. 17).

Thus, individual performance can be quantified by comparing the value of the result to a predetermined standard assessed in terms of time, quality, or quantity, and ultimately in cost. From this perspective, individual performance is representative of the effectiveness of the consequences of an individual's intended behavior. Barrie and Pace (1997) identify this "capacity to think about performance and also to perform" (p. 337) as competence, which concurs with Morf's (1986) much earlier definition. Morf defined competence as the product of "the worker's motivational dispositions and abilities that are relevant in the context of work" (p. 15) and recognized it as a performance variable.

Morf (1986) attempted to operationalize this relationship of individual performance to competence by stating that it "is a function of the interaction of the person and the work environment" (p. 113). Based on the premise that "the aspect of the worker most frequently influenced by performance is ability levels," Morf equated competence with the "new skills developed and new knowledge acquired in the very process of doing a job" (p. 14). In other words, the key element in Morf's formula for performance was actually expertise.

Unlike Morf, Gilbert (1996) saw competence not as a *component* of performance but as a *function* of "worthy performance," which he expressed as "the ratio of valuable accomplishments to costly behavior" (p. 18). Gilbert believed that worthy performance was a product of both the work environment and an individual's repertoire of behavior, or the specialized responses, knowledge, and understanding of a specific area. In Gilbert's mind, competent people were those individuals who could create valuable results without using excessively costly behavior. Gilbert defined competence as efficient behavior, and his standard of competence was *exemplary* performance, which he qualified as the "historically best instance of performance" (p. 30).

Competence can thus be seen as a displayed characteristic of expertise and a measurable subset within an individual's domain of expertise (Figure 2.2).

From this examination of expertise as displayed behavior that is effective, efficient, and measurable, the remaining pieces of an operational definition of human expertise have been uncovered. We recognize expertise in others by their demonstrated actions. Expanding on this observation, we recognize experts as individuals who do things better than anyone else. They demonstrate their acquired expertise through

▲ Figure 2.2   Competence as a Subset of Expertise

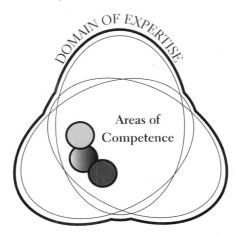

outstanding performance, and this means that they can consistently do things more effectively and efficiently than nonexperts can. Human expertise can thus be operationally defined by these two desired characteristics of displayed behavior: the consistent demonstrated actions of an individual that are both efficient in their execution and effective in their results.

Conclusion

One could attempt to argue that defining expertise adds no value because organizational performance is reflective of only the lowest level of responsive behavior, and therefore it is merely competence that promotes efficiency (Barrie & Pace, 1997). Such an argument lacks merit, for although expertise and competence are clearly linked and unquestionably similar in nature, they are distinctly different. Figure 2.3 illustrates, by its relationship to expertise, the limitations of competence as the ultimate desired outcome.

Competence can be visualized as a subset of expertise. In other words, it reflects task-specific actions and is therefore found within an individual's domain of expertise, not encircling it. In addition, competence, with its primary goal being efficient action (Barrie and Pace, 1997), can be seen as both narrowing and static, unlike expertise, which

▲ Figure 2.3   An Illustration of the Limitations of Competence

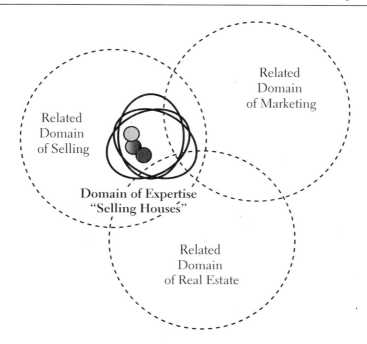

is dynamic and expanding. Competence is seen and described as an outcome (McLagan, 1997), a destination, while expertise is clearly a process (Bereiter & Scardamalia, 1993), a journey. Finally, competence reflects a specific knowledge set, unlike expertise, which despite being recognized as domain specific often extends into several related domains. As shown by the simplified example in Figure 2.3, competencies are tasks specific to selling houses, but the domain of expertise—Selling Houses—overlaps the related, but more general, domains of Selling, Marketing, and Real Estate. It is evident that organizations must look past competence and focus on the development of expertise as a desired outcome in the process of improving performance.

The proposed operational definition of expertise allows the actions of exemplary performers within an organization to be benchmarked in qualitative and quantitative terms. This permits an organization to focus on the development and implementation of training interventions designed to accelerate both the acquisition of specific knowledge and skills and the transfer of this expertise.

Human expertise is clearly a complex, multifaceted phenomenon, but by the means of an operational definition, it can be expressed in measurable terms. Human *expertise* can be defined as *displayed behavior within a specialized domain and/or related domain in the form of consistently demonstrated actions of an individual that are both optimally efficient in their execution and effective in their results.* Human *competence*, a related construct and component of expertise, can also be expressed in measurable terms and defined as *displayed behavior within a specialized domain in the form of consistently demonstrated actions of an individual that are both minimally efficient in their execution and effective in their results.*

Through the use of these operational definitions and the recognition of domain-specific knowledge, experience, and problem solving as being the core elements of expertise, organizations gain conceptual access to one of the most powerful tools for improving performance: human expertise.

References

Barrie, J., & Pace, R. W. (1997). Competence, efficiency, and organizational learning. *Human Resource Development Quarterly*, 8, 335–342.

Bereiter, C., & Scardamalia, M. (1993). *Surpassing ourselves: An inquiry into the nature and implications of expertise.* Chicago: Open Court.

Chi, M.T.H., Glaser, R., & Farr, M. J. (1988). *The nature of expertise.* Hillsdale, NJ: Erlbaum.

Ericcson, K. A., & Smith, J. (1991). Prospects and limits of the empirical study of expertise: An introduction. In K. A. Ericcson & J. Smith (Eds.), *Towards a general theory of expertise: Prospects and limits* (pp. 1–38). Cambridge: Cambridge University Press.

Gilbert, T. F. (1996). *Human competence: Engineering worthy performance* (Tribute ed.). Amherst, MA: HRD Press.

Glaser, R. (1985). *The nature of expertise* (Occasional Paper No. 107. National Center for Research in Vocational Education). Columbus, OH: Ohio State University.

Glaser, R., & Chi, M. T. H. (1988). Overview. In M. T. H. Chi, R. Glaser, & M. J. Farr (Eds.), *The nature of expertise* (pp. xv-xxviii). Hillsdale, NJ: Erlbaum.

Gleespen, A. V. (1996). How individual expertise may be socially constructed: A literature review. In E. F. Holton (Ed.). *1996 AHRD Conference Proceedings* (pp. 497–504). Austin, TX: Academy of Human Resources Development.

Hill, W. F. (1971). *Learning: A survey of psychological interpretations* (rev. ed.). Scranton, OH: Chandler Publishing.

Hoffman, R. R., Shadbolt, N. R., Burton, A. M., & Klein, G. (1995, May). Eliciting knowledge from experts: A methodological analysis. *Rational Behavior and Human Decision Processes, 62*, 129–158.

Jacobs, R. L. (1997). The taxonomy of employee development: Toward an organizational culture of expertise. In R. J. Torraco (Ed.), *1997 AHRD Conference Proceedings* (pp. 278–283). Baton Rouge, LA: Academy of Human Resources Development.

Jacobs, R. L., & Jones, M. J. (1995). *Structured on-the-job training: Unleashing employee expertise in the workplace.* San Francisco: Berrett-Koehler.

Kuchinke, K. P. (1997). Employee expertise: The status of the theory and the literature. *Performance Improvement Quarterly, 10*, 72–77.

McLagan, P. A. (1997, May). Competencies: The next generation. *Training and Development, 51*, 40–47.

Morf, M. (1986). *Optimizing work performance: A look beyond the bottom line.* New York: Quorum Books.

Pfeffer, J (1994). *Competitive advantage through people: Unleashing the power of the work force.* Boston: Harvard Business School Press.

Posner, M. I. (1988). Introduction: What is it like to be an expert? In M. T. H. Chi, R. Glaser, & M. J. Farr (Eds.), *The nature of expertise* (pp. xxix-xxxvi). Hillsdale, NJ: Erlbaum.

Reichheld, F. F. (1996). *The loyalty effect: The hidden force behind growth, profits, and lasting value.* Boston: Harvard Business School Press.

Rummler, G. A., & Brache, A. P. (1995). *Improving performance: How to manage the white space on the organization chart* (2nd ed.). San Francisco: Jossey-Bass.

Slatter, P. E. (1990). Models of expertise in knowledge engineering. In H. Adeli (Ed.), *Knowledge engineering: Vol. 1: Fundamentals* (pp. 130–154). New York: McGraw-Hill.

Swanson, R. A. (1994). *Analysis for improving performance: Tools for diagnosing organizations and documenting workplace expertise.* San Francisco: Berrett-Koehler.

Torraco, R. J., & Swanson, R. A. (1995). The strategic roles of human resource development. *Human Resource Planning, 18*, 10–21.

VanLehn, K. (1989). Problem solving and cognitive skill acquisition. In M. Posner (Ed.), *Foundations of cognitive science* (pp. 560–569). Cambridge, MA: MIT Press.

Chapter 3

▲ A Theory of Intellectual Capital

Louise Harris

The Problem and the Solution. The theory of intellectual capital has emerged in the past decade in response to the growing realization of the importance of information and knowledge. Because intellectual capital was first conceptualized during the same time period that the ideas of knowledge management and human capital became an important part of organizational discussion, now more than ever, it is essential to clarify, define, and differentiate the concept of intellectual capital. This chapter summarizes current theories and offers an alternative theoretical approach to intellectual capital, emphasizing the dynamic impact it can have on an organization.

"Information and knowledge are the thermonuclear competitive weapons of our time. Success goes to those who manage their intellectual capital wisely" (Stewart, 1997, p. 68). Many view the accessibility of knowledge as the foundation for establishing a competitive advantage in the new millennium (Edvinsson & Malone, 1997; Stewart, 1997). The theory of intellectual capital has emerged in the past decade in response to these advances within an organization. Although the theory is new and research is in the early formative stages, theoretical foundations have been identified as anchors of intellectual capital.

This chapter defines intellectual capital, summarizes existing theories and concepts, and then provides an alternative theoretical approach. Because intellectual capital was conceptualized at the same time that knowledge management became a trend in business, now more than ever before, it is essential to clarify, define, and differentiate intellectual capital. The alternative theoretical approach is used to present the dynamic impact that intellectual capital can have on an organization when it is properly defined. The dynamic theory steps beyond the boundaries of the previously identified components in hopes of being more in synch with the ever-changing demands in today's organizations.

A Definition of Intellectual Capital

In the simplest of terms, Ulrich (1998) defines *intellectual capital* as "competence multiplied by commitment" (p. 125), meaning that intellectual capital equals the knowledge, skills, and attributes of each individual within an organization multiplied by the person's willingness to work hard. Many authors cited in this chapter recognize this general definition to be the simplest and most common explanation of intellectual capital. Klein and Prusak (1994) define *intellectual capital* as the "intellectual material that has been formalized, captured and leveraged to produce a higher-valued asset" (p. 67).

The three authors who have significantly contributed to the concept of intellectual capital are Stewart, and Edvinsson and Malone. Edvinsson and Malone (1997) have defined *intellectual capital* as "the possession of the knowledge, applied experience, organizational technology, customer relationships and professional skills that provide a competitive advantage in the marketplace" (p. 40). According to Stewart (1997), intellectual capital is "packaged useful knowledge" (p. 67). More explicitly, he writes:

> Intelligence becomes an asset when some useful order is created out of free-floating brainpower–that is, when it is given coherent form (a mailing list, a database, an agenda for a meeting, a description of a process); when it is captured in a way that allows it to be described, shared and exploited, and when it can be deployed to do something that could not be done if it remained scattered around like so many coins in a gutter....
>
> The overall theory is that knowledge assets, like money or equipment, exist and are worth cultivating only in the context of strategy [p. 70].

A Definition of Intellectual Capital

Edvinsson and Malone and Stewart agree that intellectual capital is the merging of three types of capital: human capital, structural capital, and customer capital. Once an organization becomes aligned and balanced in these three foundational components, it is able to create the best possible financial capital (value).

Human Capital

Human capital refers to the acquired skills, knowledge, and abilities of human beings. The underlying concept is that such skills and knowledge increase human productivity and that they do so enough to justify the costs incurred in acquiring them (Hornbeck & Salamon, 1991). Although Becker (1964) is most recognized for the theory of human capital, Schultz (1963) was also one of the first theorists to identify the significance of human capital and its economic value. According to Schultz (1963):

> Education and other forms of human capital investment increase output in a variety of ways: by generating new ideas and techniques that can be embodied in production equipment and procedures; by equipping workers to utilize the new production techniques and initiate changes in production methods; by improving the links among consumers, workers and managers; and by extending the useful life of the stock of knowledge and skills that people embody [p. 25].

Becker (1993) defines capital as being something that "yields income and other useful outputs over long periods of time" (p. 15). Since 1964, when Becker first published his views of human capital, the theory of human capital has become a well-accepted principle: expenditures on education, training, benefits, and so forth are investments in capital. However, human capital differs in that these investments cannot be separated from the individual and, more specifically, from his or her knowledge, skills, and abilities.

Human capital theory postulates that some labor is more productive than other labor simply because more resources have been invested into the training of that labor, in the same manner that a machine that has had more resources invested into it is likely to be more productive (Mueller, 1982). One of the basic tenets of human capital theory is that, like any other business investment, an "investment in skill-building would be more profitable and more likely to be undertaken the longer the period over which returns from the investment can accrue" (p. 94).

The theory of human capital suggests that people spend on themselves in diverse ways, not for the sake of present pleasure but for the sake of future monetary and nonmonetary returns (Becker, 1993; Blaug, 1976; Mincer, 1958, 1970; Schultz, 1963). The introduction of human capital theory as an individual-oriented theory rests on the proposition that people "enhance their capabilities as producers and as consumers by investing in themselves" (Martin, 1981, p. 976). Human capital theory includes the length of service in the organization as a proxy for job-relevant knowledge or ability. A person's job-relevant knowledge or ability influences that person's wage, promotional opportunity, or type of job (Becker, 1975; Hulin & Smith, 1967; Katz, 1978).

The understanding of length of service in an organization relates back to Ulrich's (1998) component of commitment in his definition of intellectual capital. It will become significantly more important in the years ahead to recognize the commitment of individuals to an organization, as well as the organization's need to create an environment in which employees would be willing to stay. Organizations will need to create an intellectual capital environment where the transmission of knowledge takes place throughout the structure, or continue to lose important individual knowledge that has been developed through the length of service.

In summary, human capital refers to the unique values each individual possesses, which are considered assets to an organization. Ultimately, the knowledge contained within an organization becomes that organization's competitive advantage. Although human capital is often the easiest theoretical foundation to identify and describe when discussing intellectual capital, it alone cannot support intellectual capital. This necessity to connect individuals with knowledge creates the emergence of the second foundational component of intellectual capital: structural capital.

Structural Capital

Structural capital belongs to the organization as a whole. It can be reproduced and shared and is entitled to legal rights of ownership. For example, technologies, inventions, data publications, and processes can be patented, copyrighted, or shielded by trade secret laws. Also among the elements of structural capital are strategy and culture, structures and systems, organizational routines, and procedures—assets that are often far more extensive and valuable than the codified ones (Stewart, 1997).

According to Stewart, structural capital has two purposes: (1) to codify bodies of knowledge that can be transferred in order to preserve the recipes that might otherwise be lost, and (2) to connect people to data, experts, and expertise, including bodies of knowledge, on a just-in-time basis.

Because knowledge sharing is dependent on various mediums of transmission, a proper organizational structure needs to be in place. Therefore, structural capital is incorporated into the theoretical framework of intellectual capital. It comes down to the importance of connecting people with people and people with information through an effective and efficient framework of communication channels.

In relating structural capital to the theory of intellectual capital, knowledge should flow quickly and easily between functions: "Communication networks, corporate yellow pages and knowledge databases allow a company to put its best people on the front line while still keeping their expertise available to the entire organization" (Stewart, 1997, p. 124). It becomes important to understand how intellectual capital refers to knowledge and its importance in an organization. This has been defined as "experience and information that can be communicated and shared" (Allee, 1997, p. 26). Knowledge management is the "facilitation of processes for creating, capturing, sharing, storing, renewing, deploying and leveraging knowledge for enhanced organizational performance" (Allee, 1997, p 35).

"In managing and controlling the alliance [human and structural capital], human resource practices and active monitoring of knowledge flows and information requests are key to keeping intellectual capital protected while effectively contributing to the collaborative activity" (Baughn, Denekamp, Osborn, & Stevens, 1997, p. 105). Structural capital becomes a significant foundational component of intellectual capital because it provides the framework and patterns for the transmission of knowledge. In order for organizations to maximize their human capital, they need to assess their investments made in building the skills central to their competitive advantage. Hamel (1990) notes that

> in the race to learn, the initial alliance structure and governance mechanisms are followed by ongoing "micro-bargains" over knowledge access. Such day-to-day bargaining may occur at multiple levels within the alliance. This condition challenges management to construct a collaborative membrane to maximize the inflow of needed skills from one's partner while min-

imizing unintended outflows. Here management must effectively locate the interface points, staff and train appropriately, develop sound reward systems, and monitor the exchange of information [p. 54].

In order for the intellectual capital to succeed within an organization, knowledge and the sharing of knowledge need to be managed effectively. As organizations move toward a decentralized structure, leaders within the system will need to be identified. In hopes of fostering this leadership, companies are developing programs to measure, manage, and protect their intellectual capital as a means for ensuring a competitive advantage.

In the words of Drucker (1994), "only the organization can provide the basic continuity that knowledge workers need in order to be effective. Only the organization can convert the specialized knowledge of the knowledge worker into performance" (p. 68). In many cases, the knowledge worker is a front-line employee who has day-to-day interactions with customers or the end users of the product. Who can better understand how to improve performance than the knowledge worker who has direct contact with clients? Stewart (1997) and Edvinsson and Malone (1997) would argue that the knowledge worker still has limited information compared to the actual customers. What now becomes essential to intellectual capital is creating a structure that not only supports human capital but also recognizes the overall importance of customer capital.

Customer Capital

According to Stewart (1997), customer capital is the most obviously valuable component to intellectual capital. This is based on the assumption that customers support the company and its bottom line. Customer capital is defined as "the value of its franchise, its ongoing relationships with the people or organizations to which it sells" (Stewart, 1997, p. 143). Despite its significance in an organization, customer capital is often the worst managed intangible asset. Stewart proposes that most businesses do not even know who their customers are and, more specifically, who the end users are—for example, "Procter and Gamble [knows] a lot about the stores that stock its products, and [has] detailed demographic information that reveals how many men of my age and income buy its goods, but has no idea whether I brush my teeth with Crest or Colgate" (p. 144).

Customer capital, as defined by Saint-Onge (1997), suggests that the relationship of a company to its customers is distinct from that of its dealings with employees and strategic partners. Therefore, this customer relationship is of central importance to the company's worth.

Southwest Airlines has been successful in recognizing its customer capital. It engages its more committed customers in its employee recruiting process. The philosophy behind this concept is that having the customer participate in the selection process will increase customer satisfaction because the customer has chosen the service provider (Edvinsson & Malone, 1997). Other companies, such as Nordstrom's and Sears, have been successful through the application of customer capital enhancement techniques. However, Stewart (1997) suggests that if an organization does not manage to balance customer capital properly, this third foundational component will skew its intellectual capital by not properly recognizing the customers' knowledge base.

A Static Theory of Intellectual Capital

Based on Stewart and on Edvinsson and Malone's theories, intellectual capital is slowly becoming a viable alternative in building competitive leverage in today's market (Donlon & Haapaneimi, 1997; Allee, 1997) because it incorporates the foundational components necessary to do business. The underlying emphasis of this theory is the need for a consistent balance among the three theories in order to create the most optimal intellectual capital organization (Figure 3.1).

Edvinsson and Malone hypothesize that corporate value does not arise directly from any of its intellectual capital factors, but only from the interaction among all three. And no matter how strong an organization is in one or two of these factors, if the third factor is weak or misdirected, that organization has no potential to turn its intellectual capital into corporate value. Therefore, a company needs to build on these particular strengths in order to produce a higher-valued asset.

The concept of intellectual capital has derived from the human capital theory by specifically linking knowledge to capital (Stewart, 1997). By singling out knowledge from the human capital theory, intellectual capital identifies individuals' knowledge as assets to an organization. Based on this assumption, an organization needs to tap into its knowledge base

▲ Figure 3.1   Value Capital Model

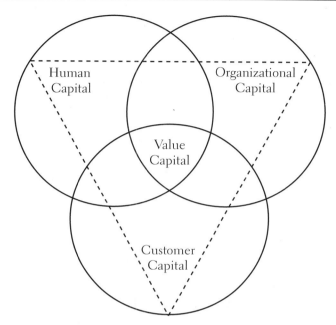

Source: Edvinsson & Malone, 1997, p. 146.

and find ways of acquiring or sharing that knowledge with others. In most organizations today, the most commonly used medium for knowledge sharing has been interpersonal communication systems. The advances in communication instruments, such as e-mail, voice mail, and chatrooms, have permitted faster, more easily accessible transmission of knowledge. The concept of intellectual capital has evolved within the past five years due to the shift in organizations to knowledge work through technological advancements.

Understanding that technology plays an increasingly significant role in the full utilization of knowledge, it becomes equally important to recognize the two distinct forms of knowledge: tacit and explicit. It is these forms of knowledge, and the transformation from tacit to explicit, that particularly suggest the overall importance of intellectual capital (Allee, 1997). The first, and more significant, is tacit knowledge: knowledge that is in the heads of people. It is the unspoken expertise that resides among individuals and teams and is often based on previous learning experiences, perceptions, beliefs, and values. Explicit knowledge is knowledge that is written down and accessible to others. Generally it is based on words and numbers and is articulated through a knowledge base, such as procedural manuals, employee guides, policies, and databases. It is estimated that 90 percent of all knowledge that an individual possesses is tacit knowledge (Allee, 1997). Therefore, companies that are striving to build and retain the intellectual capital of their organization are really striving to increase the percentage of explicit knowledge by using the tacit knowledge of others.

"Because tacit knowledge resides in patterns of relationships, information flows, and other organizational factors, joint ventures offer the opportunity for the transfer of tacit knowledge" (Baughn et al., 1997, p. 111). Organizations differ in their internal complexity and social structures, leading to different compartments for storing organizational memory. Some tacit knowledge is also based in organizational ritual, beliefs, and culture. It is conserved through systems of socialization and control as it is passed to organizational newcomers.

Experience may be embedded in the individuals and social system of the organization. This is tacit knowledge. Tacit knowledge typically involves a history of training and socialization, integration with suppliers, small-group problem solving, or advances in process engineering. It is not readily disentangled and transferred in codified form. Rather, the exchange of tacit knowledge must rely on extended social contact (Baughn et al., 1997).

The knowledge, skills, and abilities of the individuals selected for management and other leadership roles then become critical determinants of information access and how an organization and systems should be structured. "The motivation to internalize a partner's skills is further amplified if those skills can be exploited across multiple businesses and geographic markets" (Baughn et al., 1997, p. 106). Therefore, individuals and their intellectual capital must be accompanied by effective socialization (Hamel, 1990; Pucik, 1988).

The theory of intellectual capital is new, but the theoretical foundations have been in existence for many years and have helped to define human resource development today. Although the theory of intellectual capital may appear to be complex, its underlying concept is quite simple. Intellectual capital recognizes the wealth of knowledge housed in individuals and organizations and the need to connect one system with another in order to improve performance. The limited amount of research and data currently available suggests that intellectual capital greatly contributes to the success of an organization. Meanwhile, intellectual capital is slowly becoming a natural extension of organizational development. Practitioners are able to apply the concept easily and promote change within an organization, assuming the organization is ready to change.

A Dynamic Theory of Intellectual Capital

An alternative approach to the three foundational components—human capital, structural capital, and customer capital—would be to replace structural capital with systems theory and completely eliminate customer capital. Finally, the economic theory of human capital strongly supports intellectual capital and will remain a major theoretical foundation.

When Stewart and Edvinsson and Malone defined structural capital, the emphasis was placed on the "walls" of the organization and the processes within each department. Their definition even incorporates the rights of ownership that include technologies, inventions, and other processes that can be patented, copyrighted, or shielded by trade laws. Although Edvinsson and Malone and Stewart attempt to relate structural capital to incorporate the whole organization, it still has its limitations— even its title. *Webster's Dictionary* defines *structure* as "the arrangement of particles and parts in a substance or body; or something arranged in a definite pattern of organization" (Merriam-Webster, 1999). In comparison, the definition of *system* is "a regularly interacting or interdependent group of items forming a unified whole; a group or organization forming a network for serving a common purpose" (Merriam-Webster, 1999). A systems theory approach in lieu of structural capital would provide a more encompassing definition of an organization.

From a theoretical approach, "systems theory is simply a theory concerned with systems, wholes and organizations" (Ruona, 1998, p. 34). It is "a belief that the world is made up of set(s) of interacting components, and that those sets of interacting components have properties, when viewed as a whole, that do not exist within any of the smaller units" (Heylighten & Joslyn, 1992). Peter Senge (1990) suggests that systems theory also needs the "disciplines of building shared vision, mental models, team learning and personal mastery to realize its full potential" (p. 12). What systems theory does is provide a way of understanding an organization in its entirety.

By approaching intellectual capital through systems theory rather than structural capital, the organization is able to recognize its connectedness. A systems theory approach links the individual to the process and then to the organization. This provides the alignment to ensure that each person and process is connected to the underlying organization's strategic plans and business goals. Meanwhile, a systems approach would still incorporate the variables that Stewart and Edvinsson included in their definitions of structural capital.

It is important to recognize the significance of customer capital in relation to the overall success of an organization. However, by changing structural capital to systems within the definition of intellectual capital, customer capital becomes a result from intellectual capital rather than a foundational component. If an organization is truly supporting intellectual capital through human capital and systems, customer satisfaction will become second nature because it has already been recognized as human capital and then incorporated into the systems. An intellectual capital environment promotes knowledge sharing to improve performance. Therefore, the information and feedback from the customers should always be accessible and at the forefront of the organization because intellectual capital is in place. In an intellectual capital environment, the competitive advantage will become the organization's knowledge and the systems designed to access this knowledge. This would then suggest that the customers (or end users) are not the "only ones supporting the company and its bottom line" (Stewart, 1997, p. 143), but rather the individuals within the organization who possess the customers' tacit knowledge. Simply stated, if proper systems are in place for the sharing of knowledge, each individual within an organization plays an integral strategic role through the valued added by being a knowledge center for others.

This theory is best illustrated by recognizing the constant exchange between human capital and systems theory (Figure 3.2). More often than not, what is being exchanged is knowledge, but in this theory, intellectual capital is not limited to knowledge, knowledge management, or knowledge sharing.

Several companies have been quite successful as a result of adopting the theory of intellectual capital. Research on their success has found that

▲ Figure 3.2   Model of the Dynamic Theory of Intellectual Capital

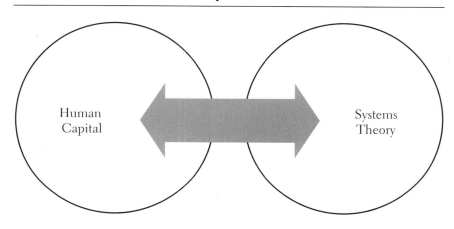

overall standards of measurement relate to human capital and systems. Although reported increases in profits suggest greater customer satisfaction, the significant improvements have been within the organizations themselves: increased retention and employee morale, greater job satisfaction and internal advancement opportunities, and overall performance and process improvements. Whenever possible, knowledge has been reduced to one transmission, and information becomes easily accessible for effective decision making.

The importance of intellectual capital, defined as human capital and systems theory, is relevant to many real-world situations. Acknowledging the importance of expertise and incorporating a proper system for knowledge sharing can only benefit an organization. Relating the theory to practice, particularly in the field of human resource development (HRD), is easy because the entire concept focuses on performance improvement.

Implications for Human Resource Development

According to Edvinsson and Malone (1997):

> The rise of intellectual capital is inevitable, given the irresistible historical and technological forces, not to mention the investment flows that are

sweeping across the modern world and driving us toward a knowledge economy. Intellectual capital will come to dominate the way we value our institutions because it alone captures the dynamics of organizational sustainability and value creation. It alone recognizes that a modern enterprise changes so fast that all it has left to depend on is the talents and dedication of its people and the quality of the tools they use.

But most of all, intellectual capital is inevitable because it alone, of any model for measuring corporate performance, pierces the surface and uncovers true value. In doing so, it restores both common sense and fairness to economics. Make no mistake, whatever path you choose, intellectual capital is our future [p. 22].

In anticipation that the theory of intellectual capital will gain momentum in both the academic and practical worlds, the HRD role will need to become more specifically defined. Intellectual capital is providing an opportunity for HRD to establish a concrete identity due to its foundation in human capital and organizational development. If HRD continues to move in the direction of systems theory, training, and organizational development, it will become a natural partner of and the strategic link in creating, developing, and supporting an intellectual capital environment. Therefore, HRD will need to become significantly involved in developing expertise through organizational development and personnel training and development.

In the meantime, companies should still recognize the human capital that does exist and work to develop each individual. Training and development should be easily accessible to all employees with appropriate means of application and follow-through. Organizations that continue to invest in people will find that the people will continue to be the best commodities for the company.

Conclusion

The competitive advantage today is no longer just the bottom line, but rather the individual knowledge and competence housed in each organization. Organizations can choose to build on these strengths and reap the benefits, or simply watch while their competitors continue to widen the gap of success. Whether intellectual capital is the answer to improvement and success depends on many factors, and more specifically, each individual organization.

Intellectual capital may indeed be the future of successful organizations, but a change is needed in the theoretical framework in order to align intellectual capital with an organization's strategic goals. The focus of this theory should be on the organization—the systems that lie within it and its human capital. If an organization chooses to incorporate this theory, the end results will prove to be fruitful.

Organizations that approach intellectual capital through the more dynamic theory will be incorporating the ability for greater adaptability, flexibility, and change. Decentralized organizations, global expansion, and telecommuting are a few examples of how organizations are becoming dispersed while capitalizing on their ability to recognize and share knowledge.

References

Allee, V. (1997). *The knowledge evolution: Expanding organizational intelligence.* San Francisco: Butterworth-Heinemann.

Baughn, C. C., Denekamp, J. G., Osborn, R. N., & Stevens, J. H. (1997). Protecting intellectual capital in international alliances. *Journal of World Business, 32*(2), 103–117.

Becker, G. S. (1964). *Human capital.* Chicago: University of Chicago Press.

Becker, G. S. (1993). *Human capital: A theoretical and empirical analysis with special references to education* (3rd ed.). Chicago: University of Chicago Press.

Blaug, M. (1976). The empirical status of human capital theory: A slightly jaundiced survey. *Journal of Economic Literature, 14*, 827–855.

Donlon, J. P., & Haapaneimi, P. (1997, January–February). Knowledge capital. *Chief Executive, 120*, 52–62.

Drucker, P. (1994). The age of social transformation. *The Atlantic Monthly, 24* (1), pp. 68–84.

Edvinsson, L., & Malone, M. (1997). *Intellectual capital: Realizing your company's true value by finding its hidden brainpower.* New York: HarperBusiness.

Grindley, P. C., & Teece, D.J. (1997). Managing intellectual capital: Licensing and cross-licensing in semi-conductors and electronics. *California Management Review, 39*, 8–42.

Hamel, G. P. (1990). *Competitive collaboration: Learning, power and dependence in international strategic alliances.* Unpublished doctoral dissertation, University of Michigan, Ann Arbor.

Heylighten, F., & Joslyn, C. (1992). *What is systems theory?* [On line]. Available at: http://www.pespmcl.vub.ac.be/systheor.html (1998, June 1).

Hornbeck, D. W., & Salamon, L. M. (1991). *Human capital and America's future.* Baltimore: Johns Hopkins University Press.

Hulin, C. L., & Smith, P. C. (1964). Sex differences in job satisfaction. *Journal of Applied Psychology, 50,* 280–285.

Katz, R. (1978). Influence of job longevity on employee reactions to task characteristics. *Human Relations, 31,* 703–425.

Katzenbach, J., & Smith, D. (1993). The discipline of teams. *Harvard Business Review, 71*(2), 114–120.

Klein, D. A., & Prusak, L. (1994). *Characterizing intellectual capital.* Boston: Ernst & Young Center for Business Innovation.

Martin, T. N. (1981). A path analytic model of human capital and organizational job characteristics on female job satisfaction. *Human Relations, 34*(11), 975–988.

Merriam-Webster. (1997). *WWWebster Dictionary.* Available: http://m-w.com/netdict.htm

Mincer, J. (1958). Investment in human capital and personal income distribution. *Journal of Political Economy, 66,* 281–302.

Mueller, M. W. (1982). Applying human capital theory to women's changing work patterns. *Journal of Social Issues, 38*(1), 89–95.

Plott, C. E., & Humphrey, J. (1996, November). Preparing for 2020. *Training and Development, 50,* 46–51.

Pucik, V. (1988). Strategic alliances, organizational learning, and competitive advantage: The HRM agenda. *Human Resource Management, 27*(1), 77–93.

Rifkin, G. (1996, June–July). Buckman Labs is nothing but Net. *Fast Company, 16,* 23–30.

Rothstein, L. (1995). The empowerment effort that came undone. *Harvard Business Review, 73*(1), 20–31.

Ruona, W. E. A. (1998). Systems theory as a foundation for HRD. In R. J. Torraco (Ed.), *Academy of Human Resource Development 1998 Conference Proceedings* (pp. 888–896). Baton Rouge, LA: AHRD.

Saint-Onge, H. (1997, November 20). Knowledge Management Symposium. Presentation at Building and Leveraging Your Organization's Intellectual Capital (conference title), Orlando, Florida. Sponsored by Linkage, Inc.

Schultz, T. W. (1963). *The economic values of education.* New York: Columbia University Press.

Senge, P. M. (1990). *The fifth discipline: The art and practice of the learning organization.* New York: Doubleday Currency.

Senge, P. M. (1998, January). The knowledge era. *Executive Excellence, 25,* 15–16.

Simons, R. (1995). Control in an age of empowerment. *Harvard Business Review, 73*(2), 80–88.

Stewart, T. A. (1994, October 3). Your company's most valuable asset: Intellectual capital. *Fortune, 130,* 68–76.

Stewart, T. A. (1997). *Intellectual capital: The new wealth of nations.* New York: Doubleday/Currency.

Sveiby, K. E. (1997). *The new organizational wealth: Managing and measuring knowledge-based assets.* San Francisco: Berrett-Koehler.

Ulrich, D. (1997). *Human resource champions: The next agenda for adding value and delivering results.* Boston: Harvard Business School Press.

Ulrich, D. (1998). A new mandate for human resources. *Harvard Business Review, 51,* 125–134.

Chapter 4
▲ ▲ ▲

▲ A Theory of Knowledge Management

Richard J. Torraco

The Problem and the Solution. Although knowledge is now recognized as one of an organization's most valuable assets, most organizations nevertheless lack the supportive systems required to leverage the value of knowledge. Because knowledge is a complex and intangible asset that cannot be managed like other resources, organizations that do not systematically examine the cultural and technical dimensions of knowledge management will experience difficulties with this task. This chapter draws on existing theory and recent empirical studies of this issue to develop a theory of knowledge management.

A theory that purports to advance the understanding of how knowledge is managed in organizations must draw from a broad theoretical base because the phenomenon the theory attempts to explain, knowledge management, is itself a pervasive concept that affects every aspect of how an organization functions. Knowledge management deals with knowledge as a vital yet intangible asset that warrants at least the level of attention given to other valuable resources. Organizations cannot afford to take a passive stance toward knowledge management in the hopes that people are acquiring and using knowledge and that sources of knowledge are known and readily accessed throughout the organization. Instead, organizations seeking to sustain a competitive advantage have moved quickly to develop systems designed to leverage the value of knowledge for this purpose (Robinson & Stern, 1997; Stewart, 1997). The studies cited in this chapter support a bold, proactive strategy for developing and managing knowledge to advance the interests of the organization.

Knowledge management has been defined as the process of creating, capturing, and using knowledge to improve organizational performance (Bassi, 1997). It is most frequently associated with documenting and codifying individuals' knowledge and then disseminating it through venues such as a company-wide database. It also includes activities that facilitate human exchanges through traditional methods such as conversations and written documents. The idea that knowledge, like physical resources, is an asset worthy of investment has roots in human capital theory. But only recently have methods been developed for sharing knowledge that are sensitive to its unique properties.

Three seminal works have brought knowledge management to the forefront of organizational research: Nonaka and Takeuchi's (1995) groundbreaking study of knowledge generation and use by Japanese companies, Leonard-Barton's (1995) detailed description of how leading manufacturing companies capitalize on their knowledge, and Davenport and Prusak's (1998) comprehensive examination of the challenges and opportunities involved in the systemwide sharing of knowledge. These works provide a realistic assessment of the cultural and technical requirements for developing a knowledge management system in today's competitive, resource-constrained business environment. Drawing on these ideas, the theory of knowledge management described in this chapter provides a complete theoretical system for effectively generating and sharing knowledge in organizations.

The Need for a Theory of Knowledge Management

There are three arguments for the need for a theory of knowledge management, each based on three of the seven roles of theory described by Campbell (1990).

Defining Applied Problems

Theory provides a means for identifying and defining applied problems. Organizations pursuing knowledge management often look for the best way to use information technology for this purpose. Information technology quickly becomes a solution in search of a problem, yet organization theory tells us that successful initiatives must be rooted in the pursuit of organizational goals. Meeting customer requirements or key business needs are core purposes for which knowledge management should be undertaken. When appropriate, information technology serves as an effective means for knowledge dissemination; it is not the knowledge management system itself. Thus, theory helps us to relate means to goals and to place information systems in proper perspective.

Evaluating Solutions

Theory provides a means for prescribing or evaluating solutions to applied problems. If knowledge management is seen as a way to achieve business goals more effectively, then the success of a knowledge management project is often defined by how quickly and effectively the business goals were achieved. However, theory tells us that the outcomes of an organization are determined by multiple factors, including the use of knowledge. The relative contributions of these factors cannot be directly inferred from success in attaining outcomes. Organizational effectiveness cannot be considered a direct consequence of knowledge management alone. Outcomes may be achieved despite the absence of best practices (enabled, for instance, by weak competition or a monopoly in the marketplace). Conversely, a knowledge management system may be quite successful despite the failure to achieve certain outcomes. Thus, theory provides the basis for assessing the contribution of knowledge management to organizational goals.

Responding to New Problems

Theory provides a means for responding to new problems that have no previously identified solutions strategies. With few precedents from which to learn, organizations implementing a systemwide project to codify and disseminate knowledge face a daunting task. Yet theory has identified the key cultural and technical variables that are critical to successful systemwide change: a clearly articulated, overarching purpose for knowledge management, top management commitment to this effort, flexibility that allows the knowledge management system to adapt to changing types and uses of knowledge, and an organizational culture that values continuous learning and improvement. Thus, theory provides the basis for responding to new opportunities for which there are no precedents.

In short, a theory is needed to keep knowledge management aligned with the organizational goals it is supposed to serve. A theory of knowledge management helps identify criteria against which project effectiveness can be evaluated, even when organizational goals have not materialized. It also provides a means for responding to the challenges of managing knowledge that are so new that they have no previously identified solutions. We turn now to the task of developing a theory to support knowledge management in organizations.

Dubin's Methodology for Theory Building

Dubin (1978), a well-known writer on theory and theory building, provides a comprehensive methodology for theory building that is particularly relevant for applied fields such as education and management. More so than other theory-building strategies, Dubin's methodology for theory building lays out an explicit road map, and it is frequently used as a template for building theories in the behavioral sciences. The methodology has eight phases: (1) units (that is, concepts) of the theory, (2) laws of interaction (among the concepts), (3) boundaries of the theory (the boundaries within which the theory is expected to apply), (4) system states of the theory (conditions under which the theory is operative), (5) propositions of the theory (logical deductions about the theory in operation), (6) empirical indicators (empirical measures used to make the propositions testable), (7) hypotheses (statements about the predicted values and relationships among the units), and (8) research (the empirical test of the predicted values and relationships). The first five phases represent the theory-building component of Dubin's model, and the last three phases represent the process of taking the theory into real-world contexts to conduct empirical research. Although theorists must consider the entire scope of Dubin's model for effective theory building, theory building and empirical research are often separated, and each of these is conducted as a distinct research effort.

A Theory of Knowledge Management

This section describes the development of the theory using the first five phases of Dubin's methodology for theory building.

Units of the Theory

The units of the theory are the concepts, the building blocks, from which the theory is constructed. There are four basic units of the theory of knowledge management, each with several conceptual dimensions of its own: creating a culture for knowledge management, a model for codifying knowledge, the accessibility of knowledge, and methods and systems for knowledge management. These units are represented by four boxes arranged around a circle, which constitutes a model of knowledge management (Figure 4.1).

Creating a Culture for Knowledge Management

Knowledge management is similar to all other important initiatives undertaken by organizations in that only those grounded in the organization's core assumptions, values, and norms—its culture—will ultimately succeed. Culture is a systemic phenomenon rooted in the organization's basic assumptions that influences the essential processes used for organizational adaptation, growth, and self-renewal (Schein, 1990). Creating a culture that supports and advances the creation and sharing of knowledge requires careful and continuous attention by leaders to the systemic issues of external adaptation, internal integration, and, most important, the development of trust among those who share knowledge throughout the organization.

The importance of grounding knowledge management in a supportive culture is evident in the experiences of failed projects that were initiated without such support. The technology to identify and distribute knowledge through e-mail, Lotus Notes, electronic bulletin boards, and other computer-based systems is now widely available. However, access to the Web or specialized software will not in itself create an environment in which people share their expertise. Organizations that were early in experimenting with knowledge management found that potential users of a knowledge management system, fearing that their knowledge may be misappropriated by a coworker, were reluctant to share knowledge in environments where the consequences were potentially negative or unknown (Davenport & Prusak, 1998). Another practice that is detrimental to the ultimate success of knowledge management is assigning the project to a department or functional area, such as human resources or information technology. Knowledge management is then perceived by

▲ **Figure 4.1 A Model of Knowledge Management**

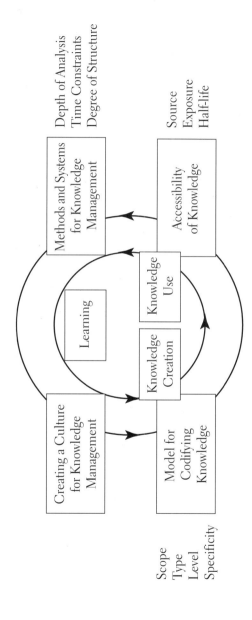

the organization as a domain of the particular department in which it is housed, which obscures its visibility as a key decision-making resource and reduces the potential reach of its benefits throughout the organization. Instead, the value of knowledge management is maximized when it is integrated with human resources, information technology, and competitive strategy (Hansen, Nohria, & Tierney, 1999). Knowledge management that is grounded in a supportive culture and systemically integrated is crucial to project success.

Because knowledge resides in employees, it should be evident that all employees, not just those charged with developing a knowledge management system, are responsible for sustaining the activities of knowledge management. While successful projects require people dedicated full time to maintaining a dynamic knowledge management system, ultimately the managers and workers who perform the organization's work (designing, marketing, and selling products; managing resources; planning new initiatives; and so on) bear the responsibility for carrying out the day-to-day activities for managing knowledge. These people must be willing to share their knowledge and make use of the knowledge of others. Leaders face a formidable challenge in creating an organizational culture that truly encourages the creation, sharing, and use of knowledge (Kotter and Heskett, 1992; Leonard-Barton, 1995; Robinson and Stern, 1997). However, new and better ideas that advance the organization's interests will not be forthcoming and shared with others without trust and a sense that the success of each individual will ultimately benefit the entire organization. The cultural foundation of knowledge management is thus an essential component of a theory of knowledge management.

Model for Codifying Knowledge

Rather than attempt to describe what knowledge is, a task that has long intrigued the world's greatest thinkers and is not yet resolved, a model for codifying knowledge is provided. This model facilitates decision making about what knowledge to share and how it should be shared. Accepting the lack of consensus on what knowledge is, the model reflects Grant's (1996) simple tautology that knowledge is "what is known" and that there are many types of knowledge relevant to organizations. The model also emphasizes the role of the individual in creating knowledge that is consistent with Simon's (1991) observation that "all learning takes place inside individual human heads; an organization learns in only two ways: (a) by the learning of its members, or (b) by ingesting new members who have knowledge the organization didn't previously have" (p. 125). The model described here is for codifying individual knowledge. The organization also supports individual knowledge creation and the sharing of knowledge among members.

The model for codifying knowledge, adapted from Microsoft's SPUD system for profiling employees' knowledge (Cusumano & Selby, 1995), has four dimensions: scope of knowledge, type of knowledge, level of knowledge, and specificity of knowledge. (See Figure 4.1.) The scope of knowledge is a four-tiered structure that addresses the range of an individual's knowledge. At the bottom level is foundational knowledge, exemplified by entry-level competencies. The next level is knowledge that is unique to a particular job or role. An information systems analyst, for example, needs programming skills to diagnose problems in the system's operating codes. Next, knowledge can be functional in scope, a level that applies to all employees in a particular function or department. All employees in the accounting and finance area are knowledgeable in financial analysis; every human resource professional would have expertise in matching employee performance with reward systems. At the top of the scope of knowledge structure is knowledge that is organization- or industry-wide in scope: knowledge of the overall business the organization is in, the organization's strengths and weaknesses, the markets it serves, and the factors critical to the organization's success.

Within each of the four tiers of the scope of knowledge are two types of knowledge: explicit knowledge and tacit knowledge. Explicit knowledge is demonstrated through expertise in the use of specific tools and methods. Winter's (1987) taxonomic dimensions of knowledge distinguish explicit knowledge—knowledge that is articulable, observable in use, and independent of a broader system of knowledge—from tacit knowledge—that which is not articulated or observable in use. Winter cites Polanyi's classic observation about tacit knowledge that "the aim of a skillful performance is achieved by the observance of a set of rules which are not known as such to the person following them" (1962, p. 49). "Not known as such" here means that the performer could not provide a useful explanation of the rules he or she followed to execute the performance. Thus, tacit knowledge, while available to the performer, resides at a deeper, unconscious level that cannot be articulated to others.

Within each type of knowledge there are also four levels of knowledge: basic, working, leadership, and expert. For a given type of knowledge, these levels can be specified in several statements that make the level clear and measurable. A person's level of knowledge can be rated by managers, peers, customers, and others who are in a position to provide informed judgments about the person's level of expertise. Finally, the specificity of knowledge is an acknowledgment that an individual's knowledge can be from a specific domain or from multiple domains. For example, a high school principal has knowledge of theories of learning—knowledge drawn from a single domain. The principal is also knowledgeable about how to foster a high school environment conducive to learning through the use of resources and incentives for teachers. This knowledge is drawn from multiple domains, including learning theory, teacher performance management, and organizational change.

Accessibility of Knowledge

The accessibility of knowledge is the degree to which knowledge is available to be shared throughout the system. The three dimensions of this unit of the theory are the source of knowledge, the half-life of knowledge, and the exposure of knowledge. (See Figure 4.1.) The accessibility of knowledge is enhanced if the knowledge is consolidated and can be obtained from a single source of knowledge. Knowledge from a single, focused source is contrasted with knowledge that resides in several sources. Knowledge that is diffused among sources, especially sources of different types (for example, people, paper documents, and electronic media), is less accessible than knowledge from a single, focused source.

The half-life of knowledge is the time interval during which 50 percent of the knowledge will become obsolete and will be replaced by new knowledge. The novelty of new knowledge gives it visibility that in the short term at least enhances access to this knowledge. Older knowledge, on the other hand, has the potential for a longer half-life by virtue of its age alone, but it must endure a longer period of scrutiny from emergent new ideas.

The exposure of knowledge is the degree to which knowledge is based on rules that are evident to the observer. Procedural knowledge can be directly inferred from the behavior of the performer (Bereiter & Scardamalia, 1993). This knowledge is easily represented by the observer from the sequence or manner of actions taken by the performer. This knowledge is more "exposed" to the observer than knowledge that is intuitive or conceptual in nature. Because conceptual knowledge is present at a deeper level, it is less exposed to observation. This is the "tacit knowledge" of Polanyi (1962).

Methods and Systems for Knowledge Management

These are the strategies and techniques used to identify the knowledge and make it explicit and available to others. The three dimensions of this unit of the theory are the depth of analysis, the time constraints on managing knowledge, and the degree of structure in the methods and systems. (See Figure 4.1.)

The depth of analysis addresses the extent to which the knowledge management system makes the knowledge explicit to others. Detailed descriptions of one's working knowledge are communicated verbally in the stories and case examples people tell about their work or in written form through research reports and other documents. On the other hand, a knowledge management system may simply identify the source of knowledge (for example, a person or document containing the knowledge) so that others can consult it directly. Knowledge mapping simply locates important knowledge in the organization and publishes this information in some kind of map or directory. The main benefit of knowledge mapping is in showing people where to go when they need expertise. Thus, the knowledge management system may present a detailed description of the knowledge itself (for example, an on-line database or direct access to a technical report) or direct the user to the source of knowledge using knowledge mapping. The depth of analysis, which is conceptually distinct from the depth of knowledge, is the extent to which the system makes the knowledge explicit.

The time constraints for finding solutions also determine the methods and systems used for knowledge management. Many circumstances allow time for search, reflection, and synthesis of knowledge. Other situations, particularly those involving customer service in which the customer needs assistance right away, require real-time performance. Methods conducive to rapid search and retrieval of knowledge are used in "help desk" applications that allow users to input data to classify the customer's problem and find a match between the problem and a solution selected from among predetermined alternatives. This real-time system delivers domain-specific knowledge through case-based reasoning technology (Kolodner, 1993). In situations not as constrained by time, methods for verbal or electronic exchange of knowledge (for example, e-mail or Lotus Notes) are more desirable.

The degree of structure of the methods and systems for knowledge management distinguishes between the methods best suited for archiving quantitative, structured knowledge and those best used for qualitative, unstructured knowledge. Structured content such as data on customers, products, prices, and specifications for service, warranty, and delivery fit well within relational database programs that give users desktop access. A database format allows information to be organized in several ways (for example, by customer or by product), with all the relevant data linked together. On the other hand, unstructured content, such as the stories and experiences of experts, are best represented in Web pages, Lotus Notes, and intranet technology, which allow users to shape their own narratives. Using a combination of structured and unstructured methods provides the flexibility to accommodate a broad range of knowledge and prevents amorphous, tacit knowledge from being destroyed by being forced into rigid structures (Davenport & Prusak, 1998). The degree of structure in the knowledge management system is determined by the types of knowledge to be represented. This relationship is addressed in the next section by the theory's laws of interaction.

Laws of Interaction

The relationships among the concepts (units) of a theory are described in the theory's laws of interaction (Dubin, 1978). Three general categories of laws encompass all forms for expressing relationships among the concepts of a theory:

Categoric laws of interaction, which state that values of a unit of the theory are associated with values of another unit

Sequential laws, which use a time dimension to describe the temporal relationships among two or more units

Determinant laws, which relate determinate values of one unit of the theory with determinate values of another unit

Because determinant laws of interaction describe specific relationships among units with determinate values, they are used in the physical sciences where such precise relationships are more common than in the behavioral sciences. The laws of interaction of the theory of knowledge management are *categoric* laws since each specifies a relationship in which one or more units of the theory *are associated with* (versus *determined by*) other units of the theory.

Wide variation in the types of knowledge challenges the ability of a knowledge management system to classify and represent knowledge accurately. Knowledge that is easily observed in the behavior of the performer can usually be represented by structured knowledge management methods such as procedures, guidelines, and other types of documentation. Yet the same methods could not be applied to conceptual knowledge that is not apparent in observable work behavior. Achieving a proper match between the type of knowledge and how it is represented by the system is the basis for the theory's first law of interaction.

First Law of Interaction: The ease with which the knowledge management system makes a particular type of knowledge available for use by others is inversely related to the type and accessibility of that knowledge.

Winter (1987) described the taxonomic dimensions of knowledge as an asset of strategic value to organizations. Winter used several dimensions of knowledge arranged along continua to describe knowledge and its strategic significance. Adapting Winter's taxonomy, knowledge and its accessibility for use in a knowledge management system can be represented along the five continua presented in Figure 4.2.

In general, a position near the left side of the continua in Figure 4.2 indicates that the knowledge may be difficult to identify and codify in a knowledge management system. The tacit knowledge that Polanyi described would fall along the continua near the left side of Figure 4.2. A position near the right side of the continua in the figure indicates the relative ease with which the knowledge management system can make the knowledge available for use by others.

For example, observability in use, the first continuum in Figure 4.2, involves the extent to which underlying knowledge is disclosed by the

▲ **Figure 4.2   Taxonomic Dimensions of Knowledge**

Not observable in use _____ Observable in use

Not articulable _____ Articulable

Conceptual _____ Procedural

Complex _____ Simple

An element of a system _____ Independent

behaviors used to enact the knowledge. For knowledge not observable in use, although the knowledge management system might identify experts who possess the knowledge, a deeper understanding of the knowledge directly from the expert would be needed by the user of the system than would be required for knowledge that is plainly evident to an observer. Procedural knowledge, on the right side of Figure 4.2, might be easily documented in lists and protocols, whereas conceptual knowledge such as that needed for designing new products cannot be documented easily through structured knowledge management methods. The last continuum in Figure 4.2, the degree to which knowledge is independent or an element of a system, establishes the relative ease of representing an independent element of knowledge in comparison with knowledge in which all other components of the system must be represented to make the knowledge intelligible. In short, knowledge near the right side of the continua in Figure 4.2 is generally easier to identify, document, and share through knowledge management than knowledge near the left side of Figure 4.2.

The second law of interaction of the theory of knowledge management acknowledges the integrity of the theory as a comprehensive system for understanding the phenomenon of knowledge management. All dimensions of a unit of the theory are considered together when determining how one unit relates to another unit of the theory. That is, we cannot take a single dimension of a unit and attempt to relate this dimension alone to another unit of the theory.

Job-level knowledge that is used to perform specific tasks provides an illustration of this law of interaction. Knowledge described as job level and domain specific may lead us to infer that the knowledge has a focused source, such as the job incumbent, and therefore that the knowledge is relatively accessible. We can simply go to the job incumbent and inquire about the knowledge we are interested in. However, the job incumbent may be a theoretical physicist whose knowledge is predominantly conceptual and quite complex. In this case, we have failed to include the tacit nature of this knowledge in our determination that this knowledge is readily accessible. That is, only two of the four dimensions of the model for codifying knowledge were considered (scope of knowledge and specificity of knowledge). The need to consider all the dimensions of a unit of the theory is the basis for the theory's second law of interaction:

Second Law of Interaction: The relationship of one unit of the theory to another unit is based on a composite assessment of the unit. The unit as a whole, not a single dimension, is considered with respect to how the unit relates to other units of the theory.

The final law of interaction addresses the role of learning in knowledge management. The value of knowledge management arises from the process through which knowledge is created and used to advance the interests of the organization. A three-phase process is responsible for creating this value. These phases—learning, knowledge creation, and knowledge use—are the basis of how knowledge management stimulates organizational innovation and growth. Learning, knowledge creation, and knowledge use represent an iterative cycle that is represented by the inner circle in Figure 4.1.

Learning is the basic cognitive mechanism through which individuals process new experiences and generate ideas. Cognitive associations and extensions form new mental representations, which give rise to new knowledge. Learning is also a collective phenomenon that is present as groups identify, create, and use knowledge for collective purposes. Learning facilitates the ease with which users and managers of the knowledge management system are able to identify, access, and contribute to the various types of knowledge represented in the system. Thus, experience and learning improve knowledge identification, access, and use. Since learning occurs in individuals, among groups, and across organizations (Kim, 1993), the role of learning in knowledge management exists at multiple levels of the organization. The integrative role of learning in knowledge management is consistent with how learning is characterized as a multilevel phenomenon by Nevis, DiBella, and Gould (1995) and Van de Ven and Polley (1992).

As desired outputs of the knowledge management system, knowledge creation and knowledge use are core elements of knowledge management. Nonaka and Takeuchi (1995) discuss knowledge creation as a process in which new ideas and information are created and synthesized into knowledge "from the inside out, in order to redefine both problems and solutions and, in the process, to re-create their environment." Knowledge use refers to the speed and methods by which organizations bring new knowledge to product and process development and commercialization (Fiol, 1996). Together, learning, knowledge creation, and knowledge use represent the iterative process through which users integrate the conceptual components of knowledge management (that is, the four units of the theory). The role of this process in knowledge management is the basis for the theory's third law of interaction:

THIRD LAW OF INTERACTION: Learning, knowledge creation, and knowledge use form an iterative cycle responsible for the dynamic process through which culture, knowledge, the accessibility of knowledge, and methods and systems for sharing it (that is, the four units of the theory) can stimulate organizational innovation and growth.

Boundaries

Dubin (1978) describes the boundaries of a theory as defining the domain over which the theory is expected to apply. The boundaries of a theory establish those aspects of the world that the theory is modeling by distinguishing the theoretical domain from other aspects of the world not addressed by the theory. The boundaries of the theory of knowledge management are shown in Figure 4.3.

The boundaries of the theory are first defined by the distinction between work activities and all human activities because the focus of knowledge management is on work. (The activities one pursues for leisure and recreation, that is, nonwork, fall outside the domain addressed by the theory.) For the purpose of establishing the boundaries of the theory, all human activities are therefore considered to be either

▲ **Figure 4.3 Boundaries of the Theory of Knowledge Management**

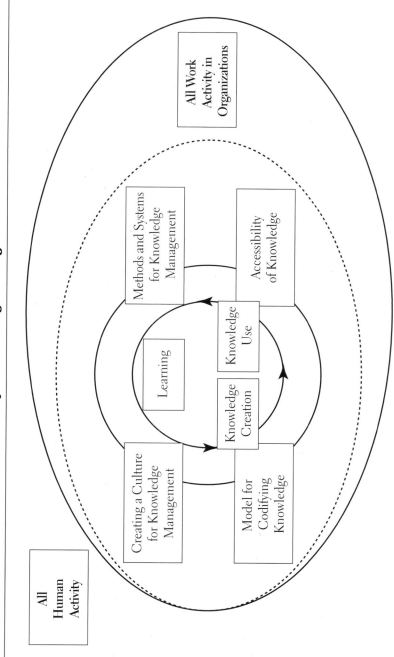

All Human Activity

All Work Activity in Organizations

Methods and Systems for Knowledge Management

Accessibility of Knowledge

Learning

Knowledge Use

Knowledge Creation

Creating a Culture for Knowledge Management

Model for Codifying Knowledge

work or nonwork. The distinction between work and all human activities separates the domain of the theory from nonwork human activities not addressed by the theory.

A second boundary of the theory exists within the domain of all work activity in organizations. Because knowledge management is used for many purposes, the boundary defining the application of the theory to the domain of knowledge management must be an open one with the domain of all work activity in organizations. Dubin (1978) specifies the use of an "open boundary" when there is exchange over the boundary between the domains through which the boundary extends. A "closed boundary," on the other hand, is used when exchange does not take place between the domains through which the boundary extends. Therefore, the boundary defining the application of the theory to the domains of knowledge management and all work activity in organizations is an open boundary, whereas the boundary defining the application of the theory to the domains of work and all human activity (including recreation and leisure activities) is a closed boundary. The open boundary is represented by the dotted line, and the closed boundary is represented by the solid line in Figure 4.3. Thus, the domain within which the theory is expected to hold is the domain of work. Within the domain of work, the theory addresses how a system manages its knowledge.

System States

Dubin (1978) defines a system state as being a condition of the system being modeled in which all the units of the system take on characteristic values that have persistence through time, regardless of the length of the time interval. All units of the system have values that are determinant, that is, that are measurable and distinctive for that state of the system. A system state that accurately represents a condition of the system being modeled has three characteristics: inclusiveness (all the units of the system are included in the system state), persistence (the system state persists through some meaningful period of time), and distinctiveness (all units take on unique values for that system state).

The theory of knowledge management is an example of multilevel theory building. Since individuals, groups, and organizations contribute to knowledge management and reap its benefits, knowledge management is expected to apply at these organizational levels. Morgeson and Hofmann (1999) call for greater precision in the description and use of constructs in multilevel theory building. Using Morgeson and Hofmann's guidelines, the particular structure of knowledge creation through learning is now discussed at the individual, group, and organization levels. The discussion illustrates this important purpose of knowledge management in the real world and thus describes a system state of the theory.

Knowledge Creation Through Learning at the Individual Level

Although learning occurs without the benefit of knowledge management systems, it occurs more readily in environments where the culture and systems exist to support work-related learning (Cusumano & Selby, 1995; Leonard-Barton, 1995). Since learning is an essential cognitive process through which new knowledge is generated, it is a necessary condition for organizational innovation. Learning occurs through reflection about concrete experience in which a preexisting mental representation of a situation is reconciled with current experience (Kolb, 1984; Schön, 1983). The learning that is best explained by this model occurs in situations where the learner has some prior experience and is therefore able to construct new knowledge on the basis of existing knowledge. In novel situations for which no prior experience exists, the learner's burden to construct understanding increases. The learner must be resourceful in using materials, local conditions, and social circumstances to construct a conception of the new situation that is intelligible to the learner. This view of learning is consistent with the theory of situated cognition in which context is crucial to learning (Brown, Collins, & Duguid, 1989). What is learned cannot be separated from the context in which it is learned. Context can include experience, but learning can proceed without direct experience. This is especially important in novel situations in which prior knowledge is limited or nonexistent. To compensate for a lack of experience and as a supplement to the context in which learning occurs, the learner relies on heuristics and abstract algorithms as a way of forming a mental representation of what is learned.

The mental representation becomes part of the context for learning. Cognitive associations and extensions form new mental representations, which give rise to new knowledge.

Knowledge Creation Through Learning at the Group Level

The group level is represented by work groups, teams, departments, functional areas, centers, institutes, divisions, or other structural units designated by the organizational system. Learning at the group level is conceptualized as a phenomenon that is consistent with Simon's (1991) observation that "all learning takes place inside individual human heads; an organization learns in only two ways: (a) by the learning of its members, or (b) by ingesting new members who have knowledge the organization didn't previously have" (p. 125). Learning is strongly influenced by context and occurs in ways that are unique to the individual. When we move to the group level, learning still occurs through individuals. As a group, two or more individuals are expected to be familiar with a common body of knowledge and the resources that are available to achieve the group's purpose. Presumably because all members of the group increase their learning about these common elements, we refer to this type of learning as team learning or, in larger systems, organizational learning. However, this is really individual learning of content that is common to other members of the group. Group learning occurs as individuals learn more about this content and about each other. However, an important issue is what responsibilities for learning are incurred by group members beyond what is already expected of the individual.

An important distinction between individual and collective learning appears at this level. Each member of the group must know how his or her role or task fits into the group's overall purpose. Methods for knowledge management, such as knowledge mapping and relational databases, capitalize on people's ability to access the locations rather than the details of pertinent information and rely on one another to contribute the missing expertise. It is the sharing of relevant data that yields the higher-order insights, generalizations, and themes associated with knowledge creation and innovation. Knowledge management helps individuals to see how their roles and tasks fit into the group's overall purpose and how to learn from others within the group. However, collective learning in cross-functional groups takes on an additional dimension: the integration of the expertise across several functional groups working together.

At this level, two or more functional groups are needed to pool their expertise for purposes that cannot be achieved by a single group. A primary challenge at this level is integrating expertise across groups such that each group knows something about what the other groups are doing. A mechanism for transferring this expertise across groups is shared mental models (Kim, 1993): representations of the world that are communicated between individuals or groups and serve as a common basis for action. Although overlapping knowledge among groups reduces the risks of omitting or misperceiving information, it poses an additional challenge: the trade-off between diversity and commonality of knowledge across groups. How much overlapping knowledge should each group possess? The risks assumed by cross-functional groups that have no overlapping knowledge are obvious: errors occur. Each group focuses on its own agenda and does not develop the peripheral vision needed for the awareness of what other groups are doing. Numerous accidents have resulted when groups fail to share their expertise and expectations of each other (Perrow, 1984).

On the other hand, too much overlap in the knowledge shared by groups creates costly redundancy. Too much commonality of knowledge may also hinder the innovation that arises from diversity of ideas. Common backgrounds can lead to low levels of attention and the absence of the diverse stimuli that contribute to innovation (Robinson & Stern, 1997). Successful cross-functional groups develop methods to determine the proper balance between the diversity and commonality of knowledge across groups. What are these methods that ensure a proper balance?

Groups that come together for the first time, particularly for innovative purposes, are unlikely to have much overlapping knowledge. Each group gradually learns more about the expertise of the other groups as they begin to work together toward a common purpose and trade interim products of their knowledge, such as draft reports, blueprints, proposals, and other work that reflects the specialized expertise of each group. As each round of refinements is shared among the groups, their overlapping knowledge increases as it approaches the point of complete overlap: the state in which each group possesses all the knowledge of all the other groups. The incremental learning of groups continues to the point at which a collective outcome that meets established performance criteria is produced: all of the learning necessary for contributing to the project has thus taken place. Although additional learning may be beneficial to a group or individual members, the ultimate recipient of the product or outcome, the customer or client, will likely not see the value of this additional learning. In fact, when the purpose of cross-functional collaboration is new product development, the time needed for additional learning beyond this point may delay goal achievement, such as the release of a new product in the marketplace. Knowledge management systems provide database archives, knowledge maps, and templates for knowledge integration to support the degree of cross-functional learning needed to achieve desired outcomes.

Knowledge Creation Through Learning at the Organization Level

Learning at the organization level includes a strategic dimension not usually considered at lower levels. This is because learning at this level must consider the mission of the organization and develop its capability for adaptation to environmental demands (Devanna & Tichy, 1990). Organizations must concentrate not only on their own operations but also on their role in the larger environment. They need the ability to identify new, potentially valuable information from the external environment, assimilate the information using the appropriate methods and systems for knowledge management, and apply it to their mission. For example, health care institutions must do more than strive to provide high-quality health care; they must also respond to a broader concern across the industry for cost containment. This concern shapes the strategy of each institution, regardless of its size or services. Each institution must learn not only how to develop its own strategy for cost containment, but develop one that is consistent with other institutions and responsive to the concerns of insurers, regulators, and employers. The scope and type of this knowledge (that is, knowledge that is industry level and tacit in nature) and the limited accessibility of knowledge (it has diffused sources and a relatively short half-life) influence how knowledge is disseminated and used within and across organizations. In this sense, these organizations must learn together how to address issues that transcend their particular interests in ways that are consistent with their missions.

Characteristics of the System State

Knowledge creation through learning occurs at the individual, group, and organizational levels. The scope of learning increases as we move from the individual to the organizational level. Because of the hierarchical nature of organizations, many of the burdens of learning at the individual and group levels are brought to the organization level, where additional responsibility for cross-functional and industry-wide learning expands the scope of what must be learned. Since this learning is cumulative—learning at lower levels is carried to higher levels—the scope of learning increases as we ascend the levels of the system. A theory of knowledge management must account for knowledge creation through learning as a key function of knowledge management, while acknowledging its unique structural properties at different levels. The description of this system state of the theory of knowledge management illustrates the distinctive characteristics of learning at different system levels that contribute to the dynamic process of knowledge creation. New knowledge for basic and applied purposes is generated when the units of the theory—creating a culture for knowledge management, a model for codifying knowledge, the accessibility of knowledge, and methods and systems for knowledge management—are considered holistically as integral elements of multilevel systems.

Propositions

Propositions of the theory are logical deductions about the theory in operation. They are true because they are statements that are logically derived from the theory (Dubin, 1978). The following propositions from the theory can then be subjected to empirical testing:

PROPOSITION 1. Knowledge management derives from the premise that systems for developing and sharing knowledge exist to support key organizational goals. Unless the goals to be served by knowledge management are articulated by organization leaders, the project will not be sustained. Like all other vital organizational initiatives, knowledge management must be anchored in important needs of the organization.

PROPOSITION 2. The importance of a particular kind of knowledge determines whether it should be included in the knowledge management project. The type of knowledge determines how it should be codified and disseminated. These are conceptually distinct issues that should be addressed in this sequence when developing a knowledge management system (that is, first the importance of knowledge, then the type of knowledge).

PROPOSITION 3. The development of trust and a common understanding of the purpose of knowledge management are crucial elements of creating a culture that supports knowledge management. The more fully a culture for knowledge management is developed, the more effective and successful the knowledge management system will be.

PROPOSITION 4. Knowledge should be standardized and edited (that is, modified by substituting common terminology) for just enough uniformity to allow the knowledge management system to work. The distinctive character of local knowledge must be preserved while making the knowledge available for systemwide dissemination.

Conclusion

Although knowledge is now widely considered to be an organization's most valuable asset, it is more complex and intangible than other resources. Systems for managing knowledge must be based on a framework for knowledge management that addresses both the cultural and technical dimensions of knowledge management. Using existing studies of this issue and Dubin's methodology for theory building, this chapter has provided such a framework.

References

Bassi, L. J. (1997). Harnessing the power of intellectual capital. *Training and Development Journal, 51*(12), 25–30.

Bereiter, C., & Scardamalia, M. (1993). *Surpassing ourselves: An inquiry in the nature and implications of expertise.* Chicago: Open Court.

Brown, J. S., Collins, A., & Duguid, P. (1989). Situated cognition and the culture of learning. *Educational Researcher, 18*(1), 32–42.

Campbell, J. P. (1990). The role of theory in industrial and organizational psychology. In M. D. Dunnette & L. M. Hough (Eds.), *Handbook of industrial and organizational psychology* (Vol. 1, pp. 39–73). Palo Alto, CA: Consulting Psychologists Press.

Cusumano, M. A., & Selby, R. W. (1995). *Microsoft secrets: How the world's most powerful software company creates technology, shapes markets, and manages people.* New York: Free Press.

Davenport, T. H., & Prusak, L. (1997). *Information ecology: Mastering the information and knowledge environments.* New York: Oxford University Press.

Davenport, T. H., & Prusak, L. (1998). *Working knowledge: How organizations manage what they know.* Boston: Harvard Business School Press.

Devanna, M. A., & Tichy, N. (1990). Creating the competitive organization of the 21st century: The boundaryless corporation. *Human Resource Management, 29*(4), 455–471.

Dubin, R. (1978). *Theory building* (2nd ed.). New York: Free Press.

Fiol, C. M. (1996). Squeezing harder doesn't always work: Continuing the search for consistency in innovation research. *Academy of Management Review, 21*(4), 1012–1021.

Grant, R. M. (1996). Toward a knowledge-based theory of the firm. *Strategic Management Journal, 17*(Special Issue), 109–122.

Hansen, M. T., Nohria, N., and Tierney, T. (1999). What's your strategy for managing knowledge? *Harvard Business Review, 77*(2), 106–116.

Kim, D. L. (1993). The link between individual and organizational learning. *Sloan Management Review, 39*(1), 37–50.

Kolb, D. A. (1984). *Experiential learning.* Englewood Cliffs, NJ: Prentice Hall.

Kolodner, J. (1993). *Case-based reasoning.* San Mateo, CA: Morgan Kauffman.

Kotter, J., & Heskett, J. (1992). *Corporate culture and organizational performance.* New York: Free Press.

Leonard-Barton, D. (1995). *Wellsprings of knowledge: Building and sustaining the sources of innovation.* Boston: Harvard Business School Press.

Morgeson, F. P., & Hofmann, D. A. (1999). The structure and function of collective constructs: Implications for multilevel research and theory development. *Academy of Management Review, 24*(2), 249–265.

Nevis, E. C., DiBella, A. J., & Gould, J. M. (1995, Winter). Understanding organizations as learning systems. *Sloan Management Review,* pp. 73–85.

Nonaka, I., & Takeuchi, H. (1995). *The knowledge-creating company.* New York: Oxford University Press.

Perrow, C. (1984). *Normal accidents: Living with high-risk technologies.* New York: Basic Books.

Polanyi, M. (1962). *Personal knowledge: Towards a post-critical philosophy.* New York: Harper Torchbooks.

Robinson, A., & Stern, S. (1997). *Corporate creativity: How innovation and improvement actually happen.* San Francisco: Berrett-Kohler.

Schein, E. H. (1990). Organizational culture. *American Psychologist, 45*(2), 109–119.

Schön, D. A. (1983). *The reflective practitioner: How professionals think in action.* New York: Basic Books.

Simon, H. A. (1991). Bounded rationality and organizational learning. *Organization Science, 2,* 125–134.

Sterman, J. D. (1989). Misperceptions of feedback in dynamic decision making. *Organizational Behavior and Human Decision Processes, 43,* 301–335.

Stewart, T. A. (1997). *Intellectual capital: The new wealth of organizations.* New York: Doubleday-Currency.

Van de Ven, A. H., & Polley, D. (1992). Learning while innovating. *Organization Science, 3*(1), 92–116.

Winter, S. G. (1987). Knowledge and competence as strategic assets. In D. J. Teece (Ed.), *The competitive challenge* (pp. 159–184). Cambridge, MA: Ballinger.

Chapter 5

▲ Training as a Strategic Investment

Richard A. Krohn

The Problem and the Solution. Leaders in the field of human resource development (HRD) recognize the need to link HRD initiatives to the strategic economic goals of the organization. Many organizations have invested heavily in training their workforce through training initiatives that can yield large returns on investment, only to see its highly skilled employees being hired away by its competition. The question being raised today is whether an organization can afford that risk. This chapter develops a model to forecast the strategic economic risk associated with investing in a training initiative.

Leading human resource development (HRD) scholars make the case that people are the only assets with the creativity and adaptive power to sustain an organization's success in today's dynamic business world. Torraco and Swanson (1995) further assert that "investment in employee education and training increasingly funds the development of an infrastructure to support the sustainable competitive advantage that a highly-trained workforce provides" (p. 13). This statement raises a question. Does investing in training always provide a competitive advantage?

According to Koch and McGrath (1996), "a central objective of the human resource management function of a firm is to enhance the firm's competitive position by creating superior 'human capital' resources, in parallel with the product/market strategy the firm pursues at any given time" (p. 336). When staffing their organizations, managers face several critical issues. For example, should they make a long-term investment in developing the people within their organizations, or should they spend more to obtain people with existing skills? When is it in an organization's strategic business interest to invest in training?

A review of the literature makes it clear that HRD practitioners must align training initiatives with the strategic needs of the organization (Koch & McGrath, 1996; Rummler & Brache, 1995; Swanson, 1994). Tools that forecast the economic return of training exist (Swanson & Gradous, 1988), but a theory-grounded tool that analyzes both return on investment (ROI) and strategic potential is missing. This chapter develops a conceptual decision-making model that forecasts the likely strategic potential of investment in a training initiative.

An assumption this model makes is that both ROI and interorganizational competitive advantage must be present in a training initiative that is strategic. If it is not, the organization should treat the investment as an employee benefit and manage it accordingly. Human capital and economic game theory provides the theoretical foundation for this model.

Human Capital: A Foundation Theory

Human capital theory suggests that investment in training should be a business decision treated in a manner that is similar to any other capital investments an organization would make (Becker, 1993). However, human capital differs from other capital investments because the investments cannot be separated from the individual and, more specifically, from the knowledge, skills, and abilities that the individual gains because of the investment. When analyzing the economics of training and development, human capital theory makes a distinction between two types of training: general training and specific training.

General Training versus Specific Training

General training is any training provided by one organization that another organization can use for its business operations. Human capital theory defines perfectly general training as any training that "increases the marginal productivity of trainees by exactly the same amount in the firms providing the training as in other firms" (Becker, 1993, p. 40).

If an employer undercompensates (relative to the marketplace) an employee with general training, the employee is likely to leave the organization (Koch & McGrath, 1996). An example is U.S. military pilot training (Becker, 1993). It is estimated that over 90 percent of commercial pilots received their initial training in the military. Because the military does not pay at the market rate, there is high turnover of pilots, who leave for more lucrative commercial pilot careers. In addition, the more widely the general training skill is known in the marketplace, the greater is the probability that a competitor will value the human capital investment and attempt to acquire it for his or her business needs (Koch & McGrath, 1996). Examples are found in investment banking and brokerage firms, where the abilities and track records of top performers are a matter of public record.

In contrast, specific training is any training provided by one organization that another organization cannot use for its business operations. Human capital theory defines perfectly specific training as "training that has no effect on the productivity of trainees that would be useful in other firms" (Becker, 1993, p. 40). An example is portions of an astronaut's training program. Outside of the space program, there is no utility for some of the training given to the men and women preparing for a space mission.

Determining whether training is general or specific is the first step in analyzing its strategic value. This, in part, is determined by labor market conditions. In a highly monopolistic labor market, an organization would have no competition for its employees. Because there are no competitors for the labor force, any training provided will have no value to another organization. This type of investment would have a high utility to the organization with a low risk of losing the investment to a competitor.

In contrast, in a competitive labor market, the training provided to the employee may be valued by a competitor. Therefore, the training provided would be general. Although the internal performance improvement potential of the training may be identical, external forces such as labor market conditions will dictate whether training is general or specific. This, in turn, defines the resulting strategic value of the training investment.

Strategic Training Investment Decision Model

Thus far, training has been presented as either perfectly specific or perfectly general. In reality, employer-sponsored programs tend to combine aspects of both specific and general training. Therefore, a model for strategic training investment must account for the entire spectrum of specific and general training combinations.

Human capital's solution to investment under imperfect conditions is first to determine the portion of the training that is specific and the portion of the training that is general. The training investment decision is then based on the expected return from the specific training (S) plus the expected return from the general training (G) minus the performance improvement value of the training to competing organizations (PI_c) (Becker, 1993, p. 44). At equilibrium the equation would appear thus:

$$S + G - PI_c = 0$$

Whenever $S + G > 0$, the training investment has the potential to achieve an internal ROI. For the training investment to be strategic, $S + G - PI_c$ must be greater than zero. When training is predominantly specific, $S + G - PI_c$ tends to be greater than zero, and it is a strategic investment. When training is predominantly general, $S + G - PI_c$ tends to be less than zero, and it is not a strategic investment.

Human capital theory asks, "Why then would rational firms in competitive labor markets provide general training if it did not bring any return? The answer is that firms would only provide general training if they did not have to pay any of the costs" (Becker, 1993, p. 34).

Human capital theory does not argue for or against training investment. It argues that investment in an organization's human capital is an economic decision dependent on many factors, including the nature of an organization's labor market. In a perfectly competitive labor environment, the human capital equilibrium point of training occurs when marginal investment in training equals the marginal return of the performance improvement (Becker, 1993). Whenever the marginal cost of training is less than the marginal performance improvement return, the organization achieves ROI from training. A question remains, Is employer-funded general training ever a strategic investment?

Economic Game: A Foundation Theory

Economic game theory is the foundation theory for strategic economic decision making. It has been called the science of strategy (Brandenburger & Nalebuff, 1996). In an economic game, the return that a player can expect is based on the structure of the game and their power in relation to the other players. Game theory provides a systematic mathematical analysis of strategic decision making in an environment where many interdependent players are making independent competitive decisions.

Early game theory proved that in a two-player zero-sum game, where one player gains only if the other player loses an equal amount, there is always a single best strategy (Diamand & Diamand, 1996). As the field developed and progressed, its mathematical analysis extended to the multiplayer economic game. In a multiplayer game, there are many different potential solutions because of the possibility of strategic alliances (Diamand & Diamand, 1996).

In many cases, game theory, because of its systematic approach, can suggest options that otherwise might never have been considered. By presenting a more complete picture of each business situation, game theory makes it possible to see aspects of the situation that otherwise would have been ignored (Brandenburger & Nalebuff, 1996). Applied to the field of HRD, it can provide an analysis of the strategic economic potential of an organization's training investments.

Competition, Collaboration, and Co-opetition

If an organization independently invests in general training, it is at risk of losing that human capital investment to a competitor. Under perfectly competitive labor market conditions, employees will go where the compensation is the highest.

In a theoretical perfectly competitive labor market, all participants in the labor pool are exactly equal. Because of this, any person employed will show the same level of return to the organization. When an employer provides general training to an employee, the labor market is no longer perfectly competitive. The trained employee will add value to all employers that compete for the employee's services. When analyzing the strategic value of general training investments, there are three scenarios to explore: interorganization competition, interorganization collaboration, and interorganization cooperative competition (which Brandenburger and Nalebuff, 1996, call co-opetition).

Competition

The first interorganizational strategy assumes perfectly independent competition. Each competitor makes the general training investment decision independent of all other competitors. The problem with this investment strategy is it makes three invalid assumptions. First, it assumes that no trained employees will not leave the organization. But those who do leave the organization will take the training with them. Because the training has equal value to a competitor, they can use it against the organization that provided the training.

Second, it assumes that others in the game will not make a training investment. Thus, the organization making the investment is assuming that it has a sustained advantage because others in the game will not make a similar investment. That is not a rational assumption.

Third, it assumes that other competitors will not use predatory performance improvement tactics. As a hypothetical example of predatory performance improvement, Alpha construction trains a person to be an entry-level carpenter. Because Alpha has made the investment in the individual, there will be a fixed amount of time before the marginal utility of the increased skills will equal the marginal utility of the training cost. Therefore, Alpha will not increase the wage rates until it has achieved a return on the training investment.

Beta construction, in contrast, did not make the investment in training, but recognized the value added to Alpha's workers. Beta's strategy is predatory performance improvement: it will offer Alpha's employees an economic incentive to leave Alpha, such as a signing bonus or a pay raise. The cost of incentive is less than the cost of investing in performance improvement training similar to Alpha's. When labor market conditions are perfectly competitive, general training provided on an internal basis is not an effective strategy.

Collaboration

The second general training strategy is collaboration. Because the utility for general training is equal for all players, one game solution is equal performance improvement.

In the example, Alpha provided general training that Beta used. If both organizations, along with their other competitors, collaborated to develop a system for general training, every organization will achieve the same level of marginal utility from the performance improvement associated with the training. There are two problems with this solution. First, there is no strategic advantage. Second, it assumes that all competitors in the market will play by the game's rules. If one of the players decides that it is in its strategic interest to use predatory performance improvement tactics, the strategic collaboration will fall apart.

The two-player freeloader problem is a classic game scenario that illustrates the problem with collaborative strategies for a commodity (Telser, 1987). The following example uses general training as the commodity to illustrate the problem with a collaborative general training initiative.

If Alpha and Beta invest nothing in general training, their performance will not change. However, if they agree to collaborate on general training, they will see performance improvement. Assuming that employees will achieve a 15-unit performance improvement gain from the training, both Alpha and Beta will realize a hypothetical net gain of 10 performance improvement units (PIU). The 10 PIU gain is arrived at by subtracting 5 PIUs of training cost from the 15 total PIU gain. However, if one or the other adopts a predatory tactic and does not invest in training, the training investment will become a strategic liability. Either Alpha or Beta makes the decision to invest resources in purchasing the other organization's human capital. Hypothetically, they will receive 12 PIU of benefit by not investing in the training (15 PIU-3 PIU of incentive pay), and they further enhance their strategic position because their competitor has invested 5 PI units into the training with no returns.

Strategically, general training is not in the interest of either employer because there is no net competitive gain. Investment in general training then becomes an employee benefit and not a strategic asset. Even though there is performance improvement, strategically there is either zero or negative gain in relation to the other player. It is in the strategic interest of a player to be the freeloader.

Co-opetition

The third strategy for general training in a competitive labor market is cooperative competition, that is, co-opetition, which Brandenburger and Nalebuff (1996) use to describe business strategies that employ elements of both cooperation and competition. The co-opetive strategy recognizes the fundamental problems with strictly competitive and strictly collaborative game solutions and offers an alternative:

It's about creating and capturing value. There's a fundamental duality here: whereas creating value is an inherently cooperative process capturing value is inherently competitive. To create value, people can't act in isolation. They have to recognize their interdependence....But along with creating a pie, there's the issue of dividing it up. This is competition.... Creating value that you can capture is the central theme of co-opetition [Brandenburger & Nalebuff, 1996, p. vii].

Co-opetition is a model for business strategy based on economic game theory. The zero-sum or win-lose game, where Beta gains only if Alpha loses, is not the only model for competition and success. Co-opetition looks for positive-sum game solutions. Instead of an all-or-nothing approach, co-opetive game solutions look for applications where two or more players can achieve greater gains when they collectively compete against the other players. The strategy is to look for competitive alliances. Brandenburger and Nalebuff (1996) developed a model for competition they call the value net. The model defines four key groups that a player interacts with in a co-opetive game: customers, suppliers, competitors, and complementors.

All of these are self-explanatory with the exception of the complementors. A player is your complementor if "your customers value your product more when they have the other players' product than when they have your product alone" or "if it's more attractive for a supplier to provide resources to you when it's also supplying the other player than when it's supplying you alone" (Brandenburger & Nalebuff, 1996, pp. 18–19). Automobile manufacturers and tire manufacturers are complementors. Without tires, an automobile is worth far less than it is with tires. Conversely, tires have less value to a consumer if they are not designed for use on an automobile.

In the co-opetive model, the complementors are the allies a player looks for to gain strategic game advantages. They add value to the product and competitive tactical advantages in the game. For a multiplayer general training game, a co-opetive strategy has the potential to both improve performance and create an interorganizational competitive advantage. The key to strategic investment is the identification of value-adding complementors that collaboratively increase the product's market value.

Using the construction scenario again, Alpha, Beta, and a number of their competitors sign a collective bargaining agreement with a local carpenters' union. They agree to fund employee general training through a joint apprenticeship program open only to the employees of signatory union contractors.

This tactic does several things. First, it adds performance improvement value to the employees that the employers can pass on to the customers. An apprenticeship program adds skills to individuals that will result in performance improvement. An employer that sells carpentry services to a customer is selling the abilities of its trained workforce to deliver a value-added service.

Second, by allying with the union, the contractors have added a strategic complementor. The union provides a pool of employees who will work for a union contractor before they will work for a nonunion competitor. Although the training is general, the value-added component of the union complementor gives the employers a strategic advantage against their nonunion competitors. They have eliminated a portion of their competition because of the union affiliation and achieved a perfect collaboration because of the binding contractual agreement between their strategic complementor (the union) and all of the competing employers who are a party to the collective bargaining agreement. Therefore, the allied employers have participated in a strategic economic game where the union-affiliated employers gain at the expense of the nonunion-affiliated employers.

As a result, the collaborative employers have created an employer-funded general training program that is strategically competitive. The resulting pool of employees have the required general skills without any single employer's bearing the entire cost of developing and maintaining an internally funded general training program and with a lower risk of losing the human capital investment to their competitors.

Training Investment Decision Model Revised

Game theory adds a new dimension to human capital's analysis of strategic training investment. The complexity of multiplayer games and game theory does not lend itself to a simple formula for identifying when co-opetition becomes strategically feasible. Figure 5.1 illustrates a four-step conceptual model for analyzing the strategic training decision:

STEP ONE: Determine if the training is strategic using the human capital formula for training investment. If $S + G - PI_c > 0$, the training investment is strategic, and participation in a coalition is not necessary.

▲ Figure 5.1   Strategic Training Investment Decision Model

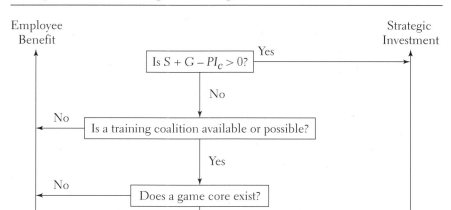

STEP TWO: Determine if a coalition is possible. For example, an employer trade or professional association represents the interests of multiple employers with similar interests and are an ideal complementor for a co-opetive training coalition. If coalition formation or participation is not feasible for whatever reason, any training provided should be considered an employee benefit.

STEP THREE: Determine if a game core exists. A basic premise in multiplayer game theory is the core (Friedman, 1990; Telser, 1987). The core of a multiplayer game is the set of solutions where each player in the coalition achieves at least as much benefit as he or she would by playing individually. Some game scenarios do not have a core (Friedman, 1990), and thus a coalition is not a rational game solution.

STEP FOUR: Determine if participation in the coalition provides strategic $(S + G - PI_c > 0)$ advantage for the organization. Each game situation is unique, and an organization must carefully analyze and question the specific nature of the game before entering into a strategic training alliance with their competitors.

It is difficult to define multiplayer game scenarios accurately without going into an extended mathematical analysis. Instead, the following questions illustrate the type of game conditions that may be encountered when analyzing the strategic nature of the investment decision:

- Is there a binding agreement among the coalition members? If there is not, then the problems associated with the freeloader scenario present themselves.
- Is the coalition stable? If the coalition is subject to fluctuations in its makeup, the game scenario can change radically (Telser, 1987).
- Is power in the coalition uniform, or is it dominated by a small group that controls a disproportionate share of the game's resources (Telser, 1988)? An oligopoly that controls the game creates a different set of solutions than a uniform power game does. Individual strategies depend on whether you are one of the high-power or one of the low-power players.
- Is the game a one-time alliance, or will it be a repeating game, where the terms of the game periodically change (Friedman, 1990)? An example of a repeating game is labor contract negotiations where the terms of the contract are periodically up for renegotiation. The one-time game is significantly different from a repeating game, particularly where there are changes in the amount of strategic game information that coalition members have regarding both their opponents and the other members of their coalition (Friedman, 1990; Telser, 1987).
- How complete is the knowledge of other players' strategic positions (Friedman, 1990; Telser, 1987, 1988)? Tactics in a game where the other players have complete strategic knowledge of your position is very different from the tactics in a game where there is incomplete strategic knowledge of your position.

Although these questions are not comprehensive, they begin to illustrate the complexity of multiplayer games. In many cases, a co-opetive investment strategy is not feasible, and a training investment should be considered an employee benefit.

Implications for the Field of Human Resource Development

The strategic training investment decision model is a conceptual tool that can be used to forecast the strategic economic value a training initiative provides for an organization. Economic game theory opens up an alternative way to approach a general training scenario. Instead of ignoring general training, it becomes in an organization's strategic interest to identify win-win alliances that result in a positive-sum game solution. Literature related to general training under different economic game conditions does not exist. This is an area in need of scholarly HRD research.

HRD practitioners need to align themselves with the strategic business objectives of the organization they work with (Rumler & Brache, 1995). Before declaring that a training initiative is in the strategic interest of the business, HRD practitioners must determine if it truly is strategic. If employer-sponsored training is going to be a component of an organization's competitive strategy, it must provide both performance improvement and interorganizational competitive advantage. The strategic training investment decision model is a tool that practitioners can use to analyze the strategic business potential of a training initiative.

Conclusion

The strategic training investment decision model is a theoretically grounded framework for HRD economic decision making. It is a starting point for answering the question, Should managers make a long-term investment in developing their people, or should they spend more for hiring people with existing skills? The model forecasts where investment in training is strategic and where it should be considered part of an employee's benefit package.

It also provides a starting point for future scholarly investigation of HRD economic theory. The combined analysis of economic game and human capital theory in the context of HRD begins to quantify the full economic impact of a training initiative. This model is only a starting point. Further scholarly analysis of general training game scenarios is needed to develop a sound theory of HRD economics.

References

Becker, G. (1993). *Human capital: A theoretical and empirical analysis with special references to education* (3rd ed.). Chicago: University of Chicago Press.

Brandenburger, A., & Nalebuff, B. (1996). *Co-opetition.* New York: Bantam.

Diamand, M. A., & Diamand, R. (1996). *The history of game theory: Vol. 1. From the beginnings to 1945.* New York: Routledge.

Friedman, J. (1990). *Game theory with applications in economics* (2nd ed.). New York: Oxford University Press.

Koch, M. J., & McGrath, R. G. (1996). Improving labor productivity: Human resource policies do matter. *Strategic Management Journal, 17*(5), 335–354.

Rummler, G. A., & Brache, A. P. (1995). *Improving performance: How to manage the white space on the organization chart.* San Francisco: Jossey-Bass.

Swanson, R. A. (1994). *Analysis for improving performance: Tools for diagnosing organizations and documenting workplace expertise.* San Francisco: Berrett-Koehler.

Swanson, R. A., & Gradous, D. B. (1988). *Forecasting financial benefits of human resource development.* San Francisco: Jossey-Bass.

Telser, L. (1987). *A theory of efficient cooperation and competition.* New York: Cambridge University Press.

Telser, L. (1988). *Theories of competition.* Amsterdam: North-Holland.

Torraco, R., & Swanson, R. (1995). The strategic role of human resource development. *Human Resource Planning, 18*(4), 10–21.

Chapter 6

 # Measuring Human Capital

Joanne Provo

The Problem and the Solution. For decades, capital has been considered the scarcest resource in an organization, and numerous financial techniques were developed to ensure maximum returns on the organization's capital. The problem is that now the scarcest resource is recognized to be human capital, and using the traditional measurement systems for ensuring maximum returns on this form of capital results only in the misallocation of resources. This chapter suggests an alternative to the traditional financial techniques that incorporates the strategic positioning of organization's human capital.

While there may be some debate over the use of the term *human capital*, for purposes of this chapter, it will be used to demonstrate that, like other assets that must be invested in to yield value, there is a return on human assets as well. A firm can leverage its human capital by increasing its collective ability to extract the best ideas and solutions from its people. Salamon (1991) uses human capital to refer to the skills, knowledge, and abilities of human beings. Underlying this concept is the notion that these skills and knowledge increase human productivity and that they do so enough to justify the cost incurred of acquiring them. Human capital theory states that "human capital is the knowledge and skills (physical and intellectual) that an individual possesses that make that individual a productive worker" (Besanko, Dranove, & Stanley, 1996, p. 641).

Like any other asset, people should be seen as a source of strategic advantage and invested in like other tangible assets. Lewis (1997) uses the accounting perspective to strengthen his case by noting a growing recognition that organizations must invest in all assets appropriately if they intend to be successful in the long term. Further, he makes the point that investing in building intellectual capital is no longer a luxury for a small minority of enlightened companies. All organizations need to do this.

Certainly information and technology are changing the way we deploy our human assets, and with this there is a need to study and explore what it means to manage the human capital effectively that contributes to organizational wealth. It is certainly not a stretch to believe that what differentiates successful companies will be their accumulation, development, and deployment of human capital. Mirable (1998) calls human assets the true measure of corporate wealth.

More and more organizations are announcing plans to manage their intellectual capital strategically and see the cultivation and investments in human capital as an opportunity to strengthen their market position (Bontis, 1996). It is important to note here that the management of human capital is distinctive from managing physical assets and that an entirely different skill set is required. Meyer (1998) takes that distinction even further by differentiating between controlling the mind and controlling the body. He says that managers are used to controlling people, but they cannot control minds. His advice for managing a great mind is to aim it in the right direction and keep it excited. This statement is evidence that the management of an organization's human assets is going to require a different set of management skills and the incorporation of an organizational strategy that provides the appropriate direction and excitement for the great minds.

The Case for Measurement

Holton (1996) stated that in order for results to occur, a human resource intervention must be "linked with organizational goals (ability), have utility or payoff to the organization and the individual (motivation), and be subject to influence factors outside HRD (environment)" (p. 15). It is becoming increasingly difficult to participate as a strategic business partner within an organization without demonstrating the value that is generated through investment in the assets that are managed. In the case of human resource professionals, that asset is people, an asset long thought to be unmeasurable. There is a need for the development of human resource (HR) measurement systems that accurately demonstrate the value of investment in HR initiatives. Walker and Bechet (1991) say that HR staff functions need to measure both efficiency and effectiveness. They note that "efficiency addresses the relationship between key results and short term human resource activities. Effectiveness addresses the relationship between key results and longer term issues and strategies" (p. 235). They further identify effectiveness as the extent to which human resources support long-term business planning and strategies. Their caution is that efficiency may not be the goal of the human resource function and provide the following example: "An 'efficient' source of new hires (defined in terms of cost per hire) may indeed be quite ineffective when many of the employees that are hired do not stay with the organization for an adequate length of time" (p. 243). Becker and Gerhart (1996) prefer the use of effectiveness measures that have natural, meaningful metrics, but they caution against the use of HR measures at the corporate level. In their view, HR practices differ substantially across the business units and facilities, and the measures may lose some of their meaning. Boudreau and Ramstad (1997) note that while HR processes have evolved from administrative activities to those having strategic significance, we have not seen a corresponding evolution in human resource measurement systems. Gray (1986) echoes the support of strong information systems, noting that it is difficult for a strategic planning system to reach its full potential without the support of the appropriate control systems.

Evidence That a Focus on Human Resources Adds Value

In a review of the theory and practice of demonstrating the financial benefit of human resource development (HRD), Swanson (1998) summarizes a number of HRD studies that demonstrate how focused and systematic HRD interventions can lead to positive returns. Delery and Doty's (1996) study also shows strong relationships between individual HR practices, such as profit sharing, results-oriented appraisals, and employment security and important accounting measures of performance. Delaney and Huselid's (1996) study suggests "that progressive HRM practices, including selectivity in staffing, training, and incentive compensation, are positively related to perceptual measures for organizational performance" (p. 965). These and other studies begin to make the case for investments in HRD. The two studies summarized next are cited frequently (Gubman, 1998; Pfeffer, 1998) as solid evidence that investments in HR lead to stronger financial results for the organization.

Welbourne and Andrews Study

The study by Welbourne and Andrews (1996) captured a great deal of attention in that it showed that an HR investment is a predictor of long-term survival and viability for organizations. The study focused on 136 nonfinancial companies that made their initial public offering (IPO) in 1988. These companies were evaluated to determine the extent to which they considered their employees to be a source of competitive value. The prospectus for each of these companies was examined and coded using the following items:

1. The company's strategy and mission statements cited employees as a competitive advantage.
2. A training program for employees was mentioned.
3. An officer with responsibility for human resource management was listed.
4. The extent to which full-time rather than temporary or contract employees were used.
5. The employee relations climate.

These documents were also examined to determine if organization-based compensation programs (stock options and profit sharing) were available for all employees or only for management.

The results of this study showed that while the companies that valued human resources were initially valued lower at the time of the IPO, those same companies had much higher values and survival rates five years later than those that did not recognize the value of human resources. The results are significant for two reason: this study clearly relates investments in people to organizational success and survival, and the financial valuations systems failed to recognize the value of investments in human resources and saw only the costs. This second point surfaces the disconnect between what the financial statements reflect and the true value of an organization.

The analysts who were conducting the valuation process to determine the IPO price saw employee profit-sharing plans as a drain on the returns that would accrue to the stockholders, and the market reacted negatively to firms that were using their capital for employee reward programs. The analysts were unable to account for the benefit that these policies would have on the efficacy of these organizations, and so they submitted a lower valuation for these companies. In examining these companies five years after the IPO, the researchers found that "a firm that has a high level of human resource value and a high level of organization-based employee rewards boosts its chance of survival to .92" (p. 911).

Huselid Study

Huselid's (1995) study was designed to be a comprehensive evaluation of the links between systems of high-performance work practices and firm performance. In this study, high-performance work practices included comprehensive employee recruitment and selection procedures, incentive compensation and performance management systems, and extensive employee involvement and training.

Nearly a thousand firms participated in the study by submitting a questionnaire that had been mailed to the senior HR professional in each of the firms. The results indicated that high-performance work practices were shown to lower employee turnover and result in greater productivity and corporate financial performance. In fact, in this study, the magnitude for returns on investments in high-performance work practices was substantial: "A one-standard-deviation increase in such practices is associated with a relative 7.05 percent decrease in turnover and, on a per employee basis, $27,044 more in sales and $18,641 and $3,814 more in market value and profits, respectively" (p. 667).

This study is being replicated by other researchers to see if the results can be substantiated. While future researchers may find varying results in the financial performance associated with these practices, this study initiated that research and broke new ground by demonstrating that effective HR practices can increase organizational value.

Beyond Evaluation

Evaluation techniques for many years have relied on the four levels that Kirkpatrick (1994) proposed: reaction (satisfaction), learning results, changes in behavior (transfer), and organizational performance. In many cases, the evaluation of an HR initiative rarely went beyond the first level. Increasingly, however, organizations are expressing an interest in evaluating the results that can be demonstrated by an investment in human capital. The organization may proclaim that people are their most important asset, but that does not mean they are not interested in the return generated for an investment in that asset.

Kaufman and Keller (1994, p. 371) suggest that evaluation techniques are often underused and inappropriately applied in organizations and identify three reasons for this:

- The most-used definitions and models of evaluation often are too restricted.
- We do not ask the right questions for evaluation to answer.
- The relationship between ends and means is not made clear in the evaluation, planning, and implementation process.

They propose modifications to Kirkpatrick's ill-defined four-level evaluation model to include the consideration and determination of the value and worth of resources, and an added level, which deals with the impact and consequences in and for society. They also support the extension of the evaluation model to organizational interventions beyond training.

Phillips's (1996) model of evaluation confronts the issue of effectiveness and performance by identifying three levels of evaluation: measures of perceived effectiveness, measures of performance, and measures of return on investment (p. 60). Although there are few HR professionals who would question the need to measure beyond perceived effectiveness, there are little agreement and very few step-by-step guides that show how to measure performance. Moreover, although HR professionals readily grasp the concept, there is not a clearly understood approach to demonstrating this value. The mistake that some organizations make is in trying to apply financial ratio analysis and measurement models to HR initiatives. A discussion of the problems arising from using these models and in particular the return on investment (ROI) methodology will be presented in the following sections.

Cost-Benefit Analysis

Swanson and Gradous (1988) presented a model and method for evaluating HRD outcomes for business and industry. Their basic HRD benefit-forecasting model and the methods that were introduced consisted of the following components: "(1) the *performance value* to result from the

HRD program, (2) the *cost* of the HRD program, and (3) the *benefit* resulting from the HRD program" (p. 21). This relatively simple and straightforward approach provided focus on performance value as the key component in financial benefit analysis.

Cascio (1987) uses the term *cost accounting* to refer to his cost-benefit approach to HR analysis. He recognizes, as Swanson and Gradous (1988) do, that performance is a key factor. Cascio introduced the use of a performance ratio to measure individual productivity and the Cascio-Ramos estimate of performance in dollars (CREPID) model to value an increase in productivity for an individual. The approach assumes that the employee's salary is an economic value of the employee's labor: "CREPID breaks down each employee's job into its principal activities, assigns a proportional amount of the annual salary to each principal activity, and then requires supervisors to rate each employee's job performance in each principal activity. The sum of the dollar values assigned to each principal activity equals the economic value of each employee's job performance to the company" (p. 182). This measure then represents the performance value, and any investment in improving performance could be measured against the cost incurred in increasing that level of performance.

Jarrell (1993) notes that cost-benefit and utility analysis are used most often to evaluate HR procedures and programs and then warns, "Using cost-benefit analysis alone, it is difficult to determine or obtain precise estimates of human resource costs and usually impossible to obtain precise estimates of human resource benefits" (p. 239). However, he goes on to say that precise estimates of costs and benefits are not always necessary where the evaluation is intended to support the planning process. Approximate estimates are useful for allowing comparisons among several alternative programs, increasing planners' awareness of the kinds of costs and benefits and in revealing hidden costs and benefits and improving the ability of planners to judge value.

Cautions in Using Financial Analysis Tools to Evaluate HR Programs

Early adopters of capital budgeting and financial accounting techniques to evaluate HR programs were sharply criticized by Hunter, Schmidt, and Coggin (1988), who claimed that in their view, "many of these methods are often conceptually and logically inappropriate" (p. 522). Their skepticism and concern were driven primarily by the definition of utility and the translation of that concept to financial analysis. Boudreau's (1983) early work on utility analysis presented one of the first applications for the use of capital budgeting as applied to such traditional human resource functions as selection and training. Boudreau believed that utility figures should be discounted and adjusted for variable costs and the taxation effect. This resulted in a definition of utility as contribution to after-tax profits. While Hunter et al. (1988) were critical of the utility model and the application to HR investment decisions, they were later challenged by Cronshaw and Alexander (1991), who argued that capital budgeting theory can be a useful framework for demonstrating the utility of human resource programs. Cronshaw and Alexander encouraged practitioners to use utility analysis models and supported the use of capital budgeting techniques that rank investment alternatives. They supported providing capital budgeting analysis of HR programs to organizational decision makers as a means of identifying relevant investment decisions. This debate is central to the issue of whether financial measurement techniques are appropriate in the measurement of human resources.

Parsons (1997) lists the benefits of using financial analysis tools to evaluate HRD programs:

- These tools help HRD practitioners to look at their programs through customers' eyes and to ask strategic questions.
- These tools guide practitioners in talking with other stakeholders about their programs.
- HRD financial analysis tools provide a rational way of making decisions.

Although the application of financial models may provide some comfort in being able to demonstrate value in dollar terms, the measures are often misapplied. Parsons (1997) recognizes this factor in identifying the limitations of using financial models:

- These tools are unidimensional; they capture only aspects of performance that can be translated into dollars and cents.
- HRD financial analysis tools have difficulty measuring aspects of performance where the feedback between action and effect is not immediate or direct.

- The analysis is only as useful as the information and values on which it is based.

Her third point is true of almost any analysis, although the values associated with people may understandably be more of a factor than the values of a capital asset. The result of using financial analysis for HR intervention is often a cost-benefit analysis where the responsibility for justifying the assumptions falls back to HR managers to defend. This propose-defend trap only leads to frustration for both professionals and line managers. The key is in demonstrating the value of investments in capabilities in a way that the line managers can understand and believe.

In their discussion of the historical limits of financial measurements, Boudreau and Ramstad (1997) expound on the danger of simply applying financial accounting measures to human resources. They remind us that accounting systems were developed over five hundred years ago to be used as an internal management control device. The direct application to HR would be the development of a measurement system that provided insight on the efficiency of HR by measuring cost per employee hired or turnover rates, but does not provide insight into the impact that HR practices have on the competitive positioning of an organization.

Return on Investment

Phillips (1996) calls ROI analysis the "ultimate level of evaluation" (p. 61) in the evaluation of the actual return in a HR program. His discussion of when to use ROI illustrates that a measure of this type is not always appropriate. In fact, there are only two areas where he finds the use of ROI calculations to be highly appropriate: in safety and health and in productivity/quality improvement.

Swanson (1998) cited several early HRD financial studies that used the ROI approach to demonstrate the value of HRD interventions. He noted that these studies "demonstrated that HRD imbedded in a purposeful performance improvement framework—and systematically implemented—yielded very high returns on investments, an ROI of eight to one or more in year or less" (p. 289). These results are indeed impressive and demonstrate the clear value of HRD interventions. Unfortunately in the financial world, high returns are generally associated with high-risk projects (Brigham, Gapenski, & Ehrhardt, 1999), and the reporting of high ROIs could reinforce the perception that investments in HRD programs are risky.

Fortunately, there is a more inclusive approach. Rather than scramble to develop the financial projections that are required to calculate the ROI, the Return on People™ approach, developed by Peter Ramstad at Personnel Decisions International, introduces a concept called threshold ROI (Provo & Neumann, 1998). This method provides an alternative approach for HR professionals for a number of reasons. First and foremost, the presentation of a definitive ROI percentage is discouraged. Investments in human resources are typically perceived to be small relative to the benefits received, and the reported high ROIs do little more than signal to management that the investment is risky.

Second, the line managers are involved and asked to quantify what an increase in performance is worth to them. This process has been demonstrated to work even for highly skilled jobs where output has been difficult to measure. The example in the sidebar on page 86 illustrates how this would happen.

Return on People Approach™

"The key to financial accounting is the consistent application of accounting rules producing comparable information across organizations" (Boudreau & Ramstad, 1997, p. 350). Given this rationale, it is a short leap to supporting the notion that HR measurement could be used in much the same way where certain HR practices could be evaluated across organizations or even across divisions in a decentralized organization. HR managers need a set of measures that appropriately account for the return on their assets: people. Boudreau and Ramstad (1997) use the differentiation between accounting and finance to differentiate between the professional and strategic applications of HR measures: "HR measurement systems should focus beyond simple descriptions of past activities, similar to traditional accounting. They should not be satisfied with measurement systems that merely satisfy regulatory requirements. Instead, HR measurement should adopt a predictive perspective, similar to finance" (p. 351).

Boudreau and Ramstad (1997) are also clear in their recommendations for applying lessons learned from financial history to the strategic role of

Estimating the Dollar Value
of Increased Human Performance

XYZ designs software products and has determined that its ability to sell and build products is a key source of competitive advantage. However, its lack of design capabilities was keeping XYZ from meeting its goals. The HR management team wanted to identify the best investments for the coming year and to quantify the impact of increasing software designers' capabilities. Return on People recommended the following approach for estimating the dollar value, or impact, of increasing capabilities:

STEP 1. People who knew the job well were asked to rank the current software designers in order of job performance.

STEP 2. The experts were asked to think about the differences in performance between people who were in the seventy-fifth versus the twenty-fifth percentile. Brainstorming revealed that those in the higher percentile designed better solutions, reached a higher percentage of milestones on time, identified synergies with other products, and provided more accurate cost estimates.

STEP 3. The experts were asked to quantify the value of these performance differences. Naturally there was a bit of disagreement around the exact value, but agreement was obtained on the minimum value of the differences by using the lowest numbers that were proposed.

STEP 4. The values assigned to these performance differences were summed, providing a total value of $80,000. Dividing $80,000 by 1.3 (the number of standard deviations represented by the difference between the top and bottom 25 percent of performers) resulted in an estimate of $61,500 as the dollar value of changing the performance of the software designers by one standard deviation.

human resources. They note that it is critical to establish linkages between business needs and HR processes and to understand constraint analysis as a way of developing appropriate and useful measurement systems. Specifically they recommend that HR professionals do the following:

- *Build on the value chain.* One way for HR to be a "business partner" is for HR managers and their constituents to truly understand the value chain and what it reveals about key constraints.
- *Search for constraints.* For HR managers to create change, they must identify and alleviate critical constraints.
- *Use data models even if the data are imperfect.* Both financial measurement and marketing measurement do not require perfectly objective information. In fact, their evolution shows that they began with very imperfect data, but with very coherent models of the value linkage (pp. 352–353).

Figures 6.1 and 6.2 show the Return on People model and the resulting benefit formula. This approach provides the business case context needed to enhance the role of human resource professionals as strategic partners.

▲ Figure 6.1   Return on People Model™

▲ Figure 6.2   Return on People™ Benefit Formula

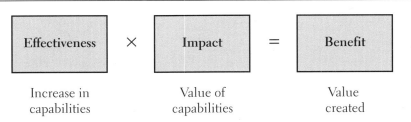

Source: Reprinted by permission of Personnel Decisions International Corporation. Copyright © 1999 Personnel Decisions International Corporation; all rights reserved.

Conclusion

It is difficult to participate as a strategic business partner without demonstrating the value that is generated through investments in the assets managed. The challenge for HR professionals is to demonstrate the value of investments in an asset, people, that has long been thought to be unmeasurable. Measurement of human capital investments needs to consider effectiveness, efficiency, and impact. Unfortunately most HR measurement systems are focused on measuring efficiency alone.

Human resource professionals should be cautioned against using financial accounting techniques to evaluate their initiatives. Financial techniques were developed to ensure maximum returns on capital, which for decades has been considered the scarcest resource in an organization. Today the scarcest resource is human capital, and measurement systems that optimize capital and not people will result in the misapplication of resources. This chapter suggests a variant on the traditional financial techniques that incorporates the strategic positioning of HRD initiatives. Application of measurement tools that appropriately leverage the constrained resource will have the greatest impact on the organization.

References

Becker, B., & Gerhart, B. (1996). The impact of human resource management on organizational performance: Progress and prospects. *Academy of Management Journal, 39*(4), 779–801.

Besanko, D., Dranove, D., & Stanley, M. (1996). *Economics of strategy.* New York: Wiley.

Bontis, N. (1996). There's a price on your head: Managing intellectual capital strategically. *Ivey Business Quarterly, 60*(4), 40–48.

Boudreau, J. W. (1983). Economic considerations in estimating the utility of human resource productivity improvement programs. *Personnel Psychology, 36,* 551–576.

Boudreau, J. W., & Ramstad, P. M. (1997). Measuring intellectual capital: Learning from financial history. *Human Resource Management, 36*(3), 343–356.

Brigham, E. F., Gapenski, L. C., & Ehrhardt, M. C. (1999). *Financial management theory and practice* (9th ed.). Fort Worth, TX: Dryden Press.

Cascio, W. F. (1987). *Costing human resources: The financial impact of behavior in organizations* (2nd ed.). Boston: PWS-Kent Publishing Company.

Cronshaw, S. F., & Alexander, R. A. (1991). Why capital budgeting techniques are suited for assessing the utility of personnel programs: A reply to Hunter, Schmidt, and Coggin. *Journal of Applied Psychology, 76*(3), 454–457.

Delaney, J. T., & Huselid, M. A. (1996). The impact of human resource management practices on perceptions of organizational performance. *Academy of Management Journal, 39*(4), 949–969.

Delery, J. E., & Doty, D. H. (1996). Modes of theorizing in strategic human resource management: Test of universalistic, contingency, and configurational performance predictions. *Academy of Management Journal, 39*(4), 802–835.

Gray, D. H. (1986). Uses and misuses of strategic planning. *Harvard Business Review, 64*(1), 89–97.

Gubman, E. L. (1998). *The talent solution: Aligning strategy and people to achieve extraordinary results.* New York: McGraw-Hill.

Holton, E. F. III. (1996). The flawed four-level evaluation model. *Human Resource Development Quarterly, 7*(1), 5–21.

Hunter, J. E., Schmidt, F. L., & Coggin, T. D. (1988). Problems and pitfalls in using capital budgeting and financial accounting techniques in assessing the utility of personnel programs. *Journal of Applied Psychology, 73*(3), 522–528.

Huselid, M. A. (1995). The impact of human resource management practices on turnover, productivity, and corporate financial performance. *Academy of Management Journal, 38*(3), 635–672.

Jarrell, D. W. (1993). *Human resource planning: A business planning approach.* Englewood Cliffs, NJ: Prentice Hall.

Kaufman, R., & Keller, J. M. (1994). Levels of evaluation: Beyond Kirkpatrick. *Human Resource Development Quarterly, 5*(4), 371–381.

Kirkpatrick, D. L. (1994). *Evaluating training programs: The four levels.* San Francisco: Berrett- Koehler.

Lewis, C. (1997). Building intellectual capital. *Management Accounting, 75,* (6), 54.

Meyer, P. (1998). Trouble finding good people: Stop trying to hire them. *Business and Economic Review, 45*(1), 11–14.

Mirable, R. (1998). Technology and intellectual capital: The new revolution. *Human Resources Professional, 11*(4), 19–22.

Parsons, J. G. (1997). Values as a vital supplement to the use of financial analysis in HRD. *Human Resource Development Quarterly, 8*(1), 5–13.

Pfeffer, J. (1998). *The human equation: Building profits by putting people first.* Boston: Harvard Business School Press.

Phillips, J. J. (1996). *Accountability in human resource management.* Houston: Gulf Publishing Company.

Provo, J., & Neumann, D. (1998, October). *Enhancing your role as a strategic partner: Defining and improving the value created by human capital.* Public workshop presented at Personnel Decisions International, Minneapolis, MN.

Salamon, L. M. (1991). Overview: Why human capital? Why now? In D. W. Hornbeck & L. M. Salamon (Eds.), *An economic strategy for the 90s: Human capital and America's future* (pp. 1–39). Baltimore: Johns Hopkins University Press.

Swanson, R. A. (1998). Demonstrating the financial benefit of human resource development: Status and update on the theory and practice. *Human Resource Development Quarterly, 9*(3), 285–295.

Swanson, R. A., & Gradous, D. B. (1988). *Forecasting financial benefits of human resource development.* San Francisco: Jossey-Bass.

Walker, J. W., & Bechet, T. P. (1991). Defining effectiveness and efficiency measures in the context of human resource strategy. In R. J. Niehaus & K. F. Price (Eds.), *Bottom line results from strategic resource planning* (pp. 235–260). New York: Plenum Press.

Welbourne, T. M., & Andrews, A. O. (1996). Predicting the performance of initial public offerings: Should human resource management be in the equation? *Academy of Management Journal, 39*(4), 891–919.

Chapter 7

▲ Knowledge Management and Strategic Planning

Oscar A. Aliaga

The Problem and the Solution. Managing knowledge has become a critical aspect of business organizations, and managers are beginning to recognize the importance of its role as a fundamental element in strategic planning. Nevertheless, there is not yet a clear understanding of what managing knowledge is. This chapter develops and defines the concept of knowledge management within the context of strategic planning.

Knowledge management and the effective use of the knowledge of the organization have become increasingly important for managers and organizations. Knowledge management encompasses the knowledge at the individual level—from individual intuition, personal networks, and improvisation—and knowledge at the organization level, which is structured, controlled, and measured (Graham & Pizzo, 1996). The final result of knowledge is improved performance, the value it adds to products and services, its impact on the definition of the organization (the "knowledge organization"), and its impact on the organization's competitiveness. Its economic value at a global level has led to the knowledge economy.

In the knowledge economy, more workers work with information rather than things; hence, they are called knowledge workers. It has been estimated that the share of American workers whose jobs involve working with things had fallen from 83 percent in 1900 to 41 percent in 1998, and that the number of people who work principally with information will increase to 59 percent by the year 2000 from 17 percent of the workforce in 1900 (Meister, 1998). To some extent this is not surprising given the nation's economic shift from the resource and productive sector of the economy to the knowledge-based service sector. In 1993 in the United States, 73.2 percent of the labor force was employed in the service sector, in contrast to 62.6 percent in 1973 (Tabbron & Yang, 1997).

The awareness of knowledge and its impact on the organization's wealth has started a frantic race among organizations in order to control it, use it, and otherwise make the most of it. Information technology experts, engineers, and managers, as well as scholars, are all talking more about knowledge and how to manage it, when to manage it, what to manage, and whom to manage it for. In that journey, *knowledge management, human capital, intellectual capital,* and *intellectual capital management* have become widely used phrases to reflect that intent and practice.

Fewer companies have adopted knowledge management systems as part of the overall strategy of the organization, let alone incorporated human resource development (HRD) in a strategic way to managing knowledge. In exploring the issue of what management of knowledge is about in an organization, we need to look at more fundamental questions: what knowledge is and what it means to manage knowledge.

Knowledge in an Organizational Context

What organizations may do about managing knowledge, and the type of systems and processes they will implement to manage knowledge, greatly depends on how organizations define knowledge.

Knowledge in the Organization

There are several definitions of knowledge. From the perspective of cognitive theories, for instance, knowledge is described based on a classification of absolute qualities. Alexander and Judy (quoted by de Jong & Ferguson-Hessler, 1996) distinguish three types of domain-specific knowledge: declarative, procedural, and conditional. On the other hand, epistemological descriptions of knowledge are task dependent, as described by de Jong and Ferguson-Hessler (1996): "situational knowledge, conceptual knowledge, procedural knowledge, and strategic knowledge" (p. 106). The complexity in describing knowledge becomes intricate because our understanding of knowledge in the context of an organization may not correspond to that of our own daily lives. Demarest (1997) has stated that "knowledge comes to us in many forms, some of which we are not able to assimilate because of our own assumptions about what knowledge is, and how it is systematized" (p. 374).

For some, knowledge in an organization is "invisible" (Lank, 1997), yet others refer to it as "a thing (object)" (Quintas, Lefrere, & Jones, 1997). Denning (1998) states that knowledge is "something that is believed, that is true, and that is reliable" (p. 4). Nonaka, Reinmoeller, and Senoo (1998) define knowledge "as justified true beliefs and bodily acquired skills" (p. 673). Fitchett (1998) defines it as "the capacity to act on information" (p. 58).

Whatever definition of knowledge is used, it is its economic value that will ultimately drive an organization to improve its performance and to profit from that use.

Intellectual Capital

Another concept that professionals and scholars use widely when referring to the management of knowledge is that of intellectual capital. However, those concepts are not the same. Bradley (1997) has provided a good definition of what constitutes intellectual capital: any idea or innovation whose purpose is the generation of ideas that can be transformed into revenues. According to this definition, intellectual capital is "the critical factor that generates value" (p. 35). Thus, the emphasis is placed on idea and innovation, two concepts that distinguish intellectual capital from knowledge.

Similarly, Larry Prusak (quoted in Edvinsson & Sullivan, 1996, p. 357) defines intellectual capital as "intellectual material that has been formalized, captured, and leveraged (to produce a higher-value asset)." Edvinsson and Sullivan (1996) themselves define intellectual capital as "a stock of focused, organized information (knowledge) that the organization can use for some productive purpose" (p. 357) that is leveraged.

Defining knowledge and intellectual capital becomes important because there is the tendency to assimilate and equate one to each other and to talk about them interchangeably (see Bontis, 1996; Greco, 1999; and Klein, 1999). The distinction and relationship between those concepts, as stated by Wiig (1997a), is that intellectual capital (and intellectual capital management) focuses on "building and governing intellectual assets from strategic and enterprise governance perspectives with some focus on tactics." Knowledge management, on the other hand, has "tactical and operational perspectives [focusing on the management of] knowledge-related activities such as creation, capture, transformation and use" (p. 400). Based on what an organization believes it is dealing with, it will develop either a knowledge management or an intellectual capital management system, or both, but with adequate distinctions and functions assigned to each.

Human Capital

Human capital is an economic concept, as opposed to knowledge management and intellectual capital management, which have their origin and application in the managerial sciences.

Economic theory explains human capital and provides the framework for discussing knowledge in an organizational context. According to the economic theory of the firm, the traditional factors of production have been land, labor, and capital. Human activity within the firm involves two levels in different factors of production: raw labor and human capital (Friedman, 1990). Raw labor refers to the factor of production labor (the physical activity for performing a task), and human capital relates to the factor of production capital (as in the case of financial capital). Economists address this distinction by calling the former "rivalous goods" and the latter "nonrivalous" (Bradley, 1997; Klenow, 1998).

The distinguishing characteristic of human capital (for example, ideas, training) is that it is intangible. Thus, from an economic perspective, human capital encompasses both knowledge and intellectual capital because both are intended to create revenue for the firm.

Value of Knowledge in Organizations

There is still a struggle for a large number of organizations to reflect the value of knowledge or intellectual capital using traditional accounting methodology. It is in fact difficult to reflect what has been called "hidden values" in the accounting books. However, there are significant and increasing examples of how to incorporate the value of knowledge in traditional accounting systems. Managers who value knowledge as a key component within the organization consider knowledge as an asset (Wilkins, van Wegen, & de Hoog, 1997).

A well-known example of how knowledge adds value to organizations is that of the Swedish company Skandia. Edvinsson (1997) indicates that Skandia developed its mission reflecting on two major paradoxes. The first is that major investments in knowledge upgrading and development of information technology led to less value in the organization (because of the short-term deterioration of profits that reduces the value of the balance sheet and therefore reduces the book value of the organization). But, second, there is a well-defined system for measuring the book value, but not for explaining the difference between the company's higher market value and the book value, in which case the gap usually consisted of the company's intellectual capital.

These traditional accounting system barriers are common. Companies cannot report training and experience on their financial statements or they cannot report the value of a scientist's ability or the replacement cost of employees' skills (Stewart, 1999). The inability to incorporate those assets poses a challenge as companies struggle to value the company's worth in the market. It is estimated that the intellectual assets of a corporation are usually worth three or four times the tangible book value (Stewart, 1999).

Management literature reports other examples of companies that have started to measure the value of knowledge or intellectual capital, among them Dow-Chemical, CIBC, Hewlett Packard, and Canon (Roos & Roos, 1997). In a survey of 1,626 managers of major U.S. companies (Management Review, 1999), 60 percent of those managers who have effective knowledge management programs agreed that intangible assets are reflected, fully or in part, in the company's market value or stock price.

Several ideas have been proposed in the literature about valuing the knowledge of an organization. One is the asset-based approach. Another links knowledge to its applications and business benefits, using a balanced scorecard "where financial measures are balanced against customer, process and innovation measures" (Skyrme & Amidon, 1998, p. 20). Roos and Roos (1997) propose a set of indicators used for each intellectual capital category that a company develops. That approach takes into account the flows between those categories and thus allows an understanding of the cause of changes—not only the end result that is obtained with the balance sheet approach. A somewhat indirect approach is the legal perspective. Intangibles are transformed into tangibles and therefore subject to valuation by the traditional accounting system. Once a company registers knowledge according to law, it becomes intellectual property. In that sense, knowledge adopts the form of copyrighted material, patents, licenses, and trade secrets (Wilkins et al., 1997).

Knowledge Management in the Organization

What is the commercial knowledge to be managed? The answer to this question depends on the organization's strategic needs with respect to either knowledge management or intellectual capital management.

In the Management Review (1999) survey, 1,626 managers were asked to define the knowledge management system at their companies. Most of them chose "creating work environments for sharing and transferring knowledge among workers" and "gathering, organizing and sharing the company's information and knowledge assets" (p. 20). Two other definitions, chosen by fewer managers, were "managing tangible intellectual capital—copyrights, patents, licenses, royalties, etc." and "leveraging knowledge from all stakeholders to build innovative corporate strategies" (p. 20). The first two responses indicate a general understanding of knowledge management as described above. The last two responses indicate that there is still confusion about the definition of both knowledge management and intellectual capital.

The Content: What Is to Be Managed

Authors have dissimilar proposals about the content of knowledge management. Wiig (1997a) indicates that knowledge management refers to the activities to create, capture, transform, and use, and Greco (1999) describes knowledge management as the documentation of "best practices, success stories, failures, customer information, and the like" (p. 20). Coombs and Hull (1998) state that knowledge management is the "shared mental framework of fundamental design concepts" (p. 242). Greengard (1998) explained that knowledge management attempts to establish "human and technological networks capable of harnessing a company's collective expertise and audience" (p. 82).

Wiig, de Hoog, and van der Spek (1997) describe some characteristics that in an organization "set knowledge apart from other resources." Among other attributes, they state that knowledge is intangible, volatile, embodied in agents with wills, not consumed in a process, and nonrival. Teece's (1998) taxonomies are tacit knowledge, codified knowledge, observable knowledge, nonobservable, positive and negative, autonomous, and systematic. Yet another classification is provided by Clarke (1998): trivial knowledge, base knowledge, and advantaged knowledge.

Demarest (1997) categorizes shared knowledge in four groups: imperatives, which are those directives that are unchallenged because they derive from the firm's dogma; patterns, described as predictive models that have "a certain longevity, durability and level of universality [and that] describe the likely shape of scenes that call for particular kinds of knowledge" (p. 377); rules, which include algorithms and heuristic; and scripts, or prescriptions for performance, which are therefore more than rules.

Principles for Managing Knowledge

Several other issues need to be covered in order to make the necessary managerial decisions with respect to the system, its purpose, and the ultimate goal of the organization. One of those issues concerns the principles that will lead the decision-making process as well as the design of the knowledge management system itself.

Davenport (1996) has proposed a set of principles that have been grouped for discussion in the following categories:

FINANCIAL LEVEL. Knowledge management is expensive (so financial decisions need to be made).

STRATEGIC PLANNING LEVEL. Effective knowledge management requires the involvement of people and technology; knowledge management requires knowledge managers; knowledge management benefits more from maps than models and is market driven; knowledge management is intended to improve knowledge work processes; access to knowledge is only the beginning; knowledge management never ends.

ORGANIZATION CULTURE. Knowledge management is highly political; sharing and using knowledge are unnatural acts; knowledge management requires a knowledge contract.

Similarly, Allee's (1997) proposed principles include those stating that knowledge is messy, is self-organizing, seeks community, travels by language, is difficult to pin down, is always changing, is a social process, does not grow forever, and is difficult to impose rules on.

How to Manage Knowledge

Managing knowledge depends on the nature of the business, the type of knowledge available, the size of the organization, and the technology used. There are several approaches to develop a knowledge management system. The first focuses on the activities it entails. Quintas et al. (1997) point out that those activities are the disclosure of knowledge, ensuring availability of knowledge at the precise location, ensuring availability of knowledge when is needed, facilitating the development of new knowledge, supporting the acquisition of external sources, distributing knowledge to those performing activities on the basis of that knowledge, and ensuring that everyone knows where knowledge is located. Calagan (1997) adds "embedding knowledge in processes, products, or services; transferring existing knowledge around an organization; and using accessible knowledge in decision making." Denning (1998) explains that knowledge management systems have two dimensions: collecting (obtaining and disseminating knowledge) and connecting (establishing links between people that know and are to know).

A second approach looks at the function that the knowledge management system has in the organization, therefore becoming "an explicitly developed and managed network of imperatives, patterns, rules and scripts, embodied in some aspect of the firm and distributed throughout the firm, that creates marketplace performances" (Demarest, 1997, p. 377). Quintas et al. (1997) have stated too that knowledge management "is the process of continually managing knowledge of all kinds to meet existing and emerging needs, to identify and exploit existing and acquired knowledge assets and to develop new opportunities" (p. 387).

Yet a third approach makes no distinctions and includes all types of purposes. For example, Hendriks and Vriens (1999) explain knowledge management at two levels: as knowledge application and knowledge creation. From a different perspective, Wiig et al. (1997) depict two important aspects of knowledge management: a knowledge management level and a knowledge object level, which are interrelated and act on each other.

A firm that is in the process of implementing a knowledge management practice, process, or system needs to be aware of several issues as it designs an appropriate system. Demarest (1997) describes six areas critical to frame the need for a knowledge management practice: relationship between culture and actions with the value of knowledge; how knowledge is created, embodied, disseminated and used in the organization; what strategic and commercial benefits are expected to be gained; the organization's level of maturity with respect to its knowledge system; who is to be organized for knowledge management; and the role information technology plays in the knowledge management practice.

There are also focus areas that are critical from the systemic and managerial perspectives. Wiig (1997b) identifies four of them: top-down monitoring and facilitation of knowledge-related activities; creation and maintenance of knowledge infrastructure; renewing, organizing, and transferring knowledge assets; and leveraging knowledge assets to realize their value.

The Strategic Nature of Managing Knowledge: A Role for Human Resource Development

HRD, through both training and organization development, becomes a key partner in the strategic use of knowledge and in the overall strategic planning process.

Torraco and Swanson have consistently presented the case for the strategic roles of HRD in organizations (Torraco & Swanson, 1995, 1997; Swanson, 1994, 1999). Within this call, it has been recognized that the overall primary role of managing knowledge is to "increase the quality and quantity of marketplace performance: to enable the firm to sell more and sell better, to support more and support better, to create and keep more, better, customers" (Demarest, 1997, p. 379). What that statement reveals is that knowledge management is a key component of an organization's strategy.

Describing the overall strategic role of knowledge management and intellectual capital, Wiig (1997a) proposes a distinction between these two concepts and states that the former is meant to support the creativity of intellectual capital. He deems this as tactical support: "Knowledge management has tactical and operational perspectives. Knowledge management is more detailed and focuses on facilitating and managing knowledge-related activities.... Its function is to plan, implement, operate and monitor all the knowledge-related activities and programs required for effective intellectual capital management" (p. 400). In that definition resides a subordinate conceptualization of knowledge management with respect to intellectual capital management, but it also recognizes its strategic role.

That perception is crucial to relate intellectual capital management, and knowledge management, to the creation and sustainability of core competencies as defined by Prahalad and Hamel (1990). The strategic role of an organizational system to manage knowledge (that is, knowledge management or intellectual capital management) serves to envision the future of the organization. The development of that vision and core competencies will give the company the required competitive advantage. "In order to sustain competitive advantage firms need to possess resources which are unique and which are difficult for competitors to capture through transfer or imitation" (Jordan & Jones, 1997, p. 392). It is in the development of the competitive advantage that the role of HRD as a discipline becomes more important.

The implementation of a strategic system for managing knowledge in an organization has many implications for HRD. Some of those implications relate to the strategic area, where HRD has to be aligned with the overall strategy of the company. That alignment derives from the need for working in increasingly more self-managed teams that themselves are the result of managing knowledge and technology advances. These self-managed teams are in contrast to what happened in the mass-production economy, which required 20 percent of highly educated people to manage the remaining 80 percent (Tabbron & Yang, 1997).

Another crucial area for HRD is the need to focus on removing organizational barriers to creativity (Lusch, Harvey, & Speier, 1998), which means facilitating changes in the organization's culture and values. "If the specialist skills and knowledge of the individuals can be efficiently accessed and harnessed, then it is possible to develop a sustainable position which is extremely difficult for competitors to imitate" (Jordan & Jones, 1997, p. 393). Mullin (1996) reports the impact that knowledge management has in changing the working culture in organizations and indicates that "companies generally can't handle the culture change involved" (p. 56).

In the same manner, HRD intervention is key in leveraging knowledge among personnel. This leveraging comes from providing training, but also from evaluating the overall organization's needs to deploy human resource capabilities and knowledge. "The trick to managing knowledge is developing a staff with the ability to know what information creates value" (Mullin, 1996, p. 56). Technology is an important component that enables the management of knowledge, but the key players are still individuals within the organizations.

Therefore, the HRD role is important due to the nature of the discipline and its function in managing knowledge to improve performance and increase value.

Conclusion

In 1991, Ikujiro Nonaka said, "In an economy where the only certainty is uncertainty, the one sure source of lasting competitive advantage is knowledge" (Greco, 1999, p. 19). Beyond that definition, and given the current state of economics and business management, there is the fact that companies increasingly have adopted knowledge management practices of various sorts. Davenport (1996) reports that Buckman Laboratories spends 3.5 percent of its revenues on knowledge management and that McKinsey & Co. has long had an objective of spending 10 percent of its revenues on developing and managing intellectual capital.

A recent survey reported that 18.5 percent of managers of the companies interviewed had a formal knowledge management program in place (Management Review, 1999). That number reveals that the majority of companies have not yet explored one of today's most important assets: knowledge.

In a fast-moving economy, managing knowledge becomes a key strategic element, and HRD professionals have an opportunity to support the strategic positioning of firms.

References

Allee, V. (1997, November). Twelve principles of knowledge management. *Training and Development, 51*(11), 71–74.

Bontis, N. (1996). There's a price on your head: Managing intellectual capital strategically. *Business Quarterly, 60*(4), 40–46.

Bradley, K. (1997). Intellectual capital and the new wealth of nations II. *Business Strategy Review,* 8(4), 33–44.

Calagan, P. A. (1997, December). Smart companies. *Training and Development,* 51(12), 20–24.

Clarke, P. (1998). Implementing a knowledge strategy for your firm. *Research Technology Management,* 41(2), 28–31.

Coombs, R., & Hull, R. (1998). "Knowledge management practices" and path-dependency in innovation. *Research Policy,* 27, 237–253.

Davenport, T. H. (1996). Some principles of knowledge management. *Strategy and Business.* Available at: http://www.strategy-business.com/strategy/96105/.

De Jong, T., & Ferguson-Hessler M. G. M. (1996). Types and qualities of knowledge. *Educational Psychologist,* 31 (2), 105–113.

Demarest, M. (1997). Understanding knowledge management. *Long Range Planning,* 30, 374–384.

Denning, S. (1998, October). *What is knowledge management?* Background paper for the World Development Report. Washington, DC: World Bank.

Edvinsson, L. (1997). Developing intellectual capital at Skandia. *Long Range Planning,* 30, 366–373.

Edvinsson, L., & Sullivan, P. (1996). Developing a model for managing intellectual capital. *European Management Journal,* 14, 356–364.

Fitchett, J. (1998). Managing your organization's key asset: Knowledge. *Healthcare Forum Journal,* 41(3), 56–60.

Friedman, D. D. (1990). *Price theory: An intermediate text* (2nd ed.). Cincinnati, OH: South-Western Publishing.

Graham, A. B., & Pizzo, V. G. (1996). A question of balance: Case studies in strategic knowledge management. *European Management Journal,* 14, 338–346.

Greco, J. (1999). Knowledge is power. *Journal of Business Strategy,* 20(2), 18–22.

Greengard, S. (1998). Storing, shaping and sharing collective wisdom. *Workforce,* 77(10), 82–87.

Hendriks, P. H. J., & Vriens, D. J. (1999). Knowledge-based systems and knowledge management: Friends or foes? *Information and Management,* 35, 113–125.

Jordan, J., & Jones, P. (1997). Assessing your company's knowledge management style. *Long Range Planning,* 30, 392–398.

Klein, M. (1999, March 29). Managing knowledge drives key decisions. *National Underwriter, 103*(13), 17, 19.

Klenow, P. J. (1998). Ideas versus rival human capital: Industry evidence on growth models. *Journal of Monetary Economics, 42,* 3–23.

Lank, E. (1997). Leveraging invisible assets: The human factor. *Long Range Planning, 30,* 406–412.

Lusch, R. F., Harvey, M., & Speier, C. (1998). ROI[3]: The building blocks for successful global organizations in the 21st Century. *European Management Journal, 16,* 714–728.

Management Review. (1999). Survey on knowledge management. *Management Review, 88*(4), 20–23.

Meister, J. C. (1998). *Corporate universities: Lessons in building a world-class work force.* New York: McGraw-Hill.

Mullin, R. (1996). Knowledge management: A cultural evolution. *Journal of Business Strategy, 17*(5), 56–59.

Nonaka, I., Reinmoeller, P., & Senoo, D. (1998). The "ART" of knowledge: Systems to capitalize on market knowledge. *European Management Journal, 16,* 673–684.

Prahalad, C. K., & Hamel, G. (1990). The core competence of the corporation. *Harvard Business Review, 68*(3), 79–91.

Quintas, P., Lefrere, P., & Jones, G. (1997). Knowledge management: A strategic agenda. *Long Range Planning, 30,* 385–391.

Roos, G., & Roos, J. (1997). Measuring your company's intellectual performance. *Long Range Planning, 30,* 413–426.

Skyrme, D. J., & Amidon, D. M. (1998). New measures of success. *Journal of Business Strategy, 19,* 20–24.

Stewart, T. A. (1999). *Intellectual capital: The new wealth of organizations.* New York: Currency Doubleday.

Swanson, R. A. (1994). *Analysis for improving performance.* San Francisco: Berrett-Koehler.

Swanson, R. A. (1999, October 6). *Strategic roles of human resource development in the new millennium.* Keynote presentation for the launch of the South African Academy of Human Resource Development, Johannesburg, South Africa.

Tabbron, G., & Yang, J. (1997). The interaction between technical and vocational education and training (TVET) and economic development in advanced countries. *International Journal of Educational Development, 17,* 323–334.

Teece, D. J. (1998). Capturing value from knowledge assets: The new economy, markets for know-how, and intangible assets. *California Management Review, 40*(3), 55–79.

Torraco, R. J., & Swanson, R. A. (1995). The strategic roles of human resource development *Human Resource Planning, 18*(4), pp. 10–21.

Torraco, R. J. & Swanson, R. A. (1997). The strategic audit of HRD as a change intervention. In E. Holton (Ed.), *Leading organizational change* (pp. 99–121). Alexandria, VA: ASTD Press.

Wiig, K. M. (1997a). Integrating intellectual capital and knowledge management. *Long Range Planning, 30,* 399–405.

Wiig, K. M. (1997b). Knowledge management: Where did it come from and where will it go? *Expert Systems with Applications, 13,* 1–14.

Wiig, K. M., de Hoog, R., & van der Spek, R. (1997). Supporting knowledge management: A selection of methods and techniques. *Expert Systems with Applications, 13,* 15–27.

Wilkins, J., van Wegen, B., & de Hoog, R. (1997). Understanding and valuing knowledge assets: Overview and method. *Expert Systems with Applications, 13,* 55–72.

Index

▲ ▲ ▲

The Authors

Oscar A. Aliaga, a Peruvian attorney, has worked extensively in research on conflict management and organization development at the Conflict and Change Center, University of Minnesota. His areas of interest include human capital theory, knowledge management, training and diversity, strategic human resource development (HRD), and foreign investment and HRD. He is a research associate and adjunct faculty member at the University of Minnesota and Ph.D. candidate in HRD.

Louise Harris is the manager of organizational effectiveness at Deluxe Corporation, where she is responsible for executive leadership development, succession planning, and organizational capital efforts. Harris is also a Ph.D. student in HRD at the University of Minnesota, where her focus is on intellectual capital, knowledge management, and systems thinking.

Richard W. Herling is the principal training consultant and training business unit manager for Metsys Engineering, a consulting group that develops customized training programs and materials focused on developing worker expertise and improving performance. Herling is also a doctoral student in the University of Minnesota's human resource development program, where the focus of his research has been on the development of organizational expertise.

Richard A. Krohn is director of workforce development for the Minnesota chapter of the Associated General Contractors of America. Prior to this, he worked for an international general contractor in a number of different management roles, including corporate safety director and technical training manager. Krohn is also a doctoral student in the University of Minnesota's Human Resource Development program.

Joanne Provo leads a practice area at Personnel Decisions International that focuses on human capital strategy and measurement. Her research interests are human capital strategy and demonstrating the impact that

HRD investments have on value creation for organizations. Provo received her Ph.D. degree in human resource development from the University of Minnesota.

Richard J. Torraco is assistant professor of human resource development in the Department of Educational Administration at the University of Nebraska-Lincoln. Torraco also coordinates the HRD graduate program at the University of Nebraska. His research activities include theory building in HRD, HRD and performance improvement, and the changing nature of work and careers.

Academy of Human Resource Development

The Academy of Human Resource Development (AHRD) is a global organization made up of, governed by, and created for the human resource development (HRD) scholarly community of academics and reflective practitioners. The Academy was formed to encourage systematic study of human resource development theories, processes, and practices; to disseminate information about HRD; to encourage the application of HRD research findings; and to provide opportunities for social interaction among individuals with scholarly and professional interests in HRD from multiple disciplines and from across the globe.

AHRD membership includes a subscription to *Advances in Developing Human Resources, Human Resource Development Quarterly,* and *Human Resource Development International.* A partial list of other benefits includes (1) membership in the only global organization dedicated to advancing the HRD profession through research, (2) annual research conference with full proceedings of research papers (900 pages), (3) reduced prices on professional books, (4) subscription to the *Forum,* the academy newsletter, and (5) research partnering, funding, and publishing opportunities. Senior practitioners are encouraged to join AHRD's Global 100!

> Academy of Human Resource Development
> P.O. Box 25113
> Baton Rouge, LA 70894-5111
> USA
>
> Phone: 225-334-1874
> Fax: 225-334-1875
> E-mail: office@ahrd.org
> Website: http://www.ahrd.org

Check out Berrett-Koehler's new website:
www.bkconnection.com

✔ Special Internet-only discounts
✔ Pre-publication previews of new books
✔ Exclusive articles available only on our site
✔ And more!

BERRETT-KOEHLER is pleased to announce the launch of our new website at www.bkconnection.com. One of our primary purposes at Berrett-Koehler has been to build and sustain a community of readers, customers, and other stakeholders who are committed to creating a more enlightened world of work and more open, effective, and humane organizations. We have created this website to serve as a hub for that community. This new site features:

Advance previews and special discounts
- Savings of up to 30% on new releases and special offers
- The latest e-commerce technology which ensures safe and secure online ordering
- A complete catalog—everything we've ever published, searchable by author and title
- Excerpts from new and forthcoming books: Currently we are featuring a preview of the new, revised and expanded edition of Margaret Wheatley's classic *Leadership and the New Science*. If you haven't read it, find out why the first edition sold over 200,000 copies and was named one of the top ten books of the past decade by *CIO Magazine* and one of the top ten business books of all time by Xerox Business Services. If you have read it, find out what's new in the revised and expanded edition, share your thoughts about the book with other readers, and discover how you can start a *Leadership and the New Science* discussion group.

Exclusive information available nowhere else
- "Think Tank," a section featuring articles by some of the most innovative thinkers in business today—including Alan Briskin, Hazel Henderson, Barbara Moses, Sam Stern, and many others
- A "Tip-of-the-Week" section where you'll find practical tips from renowned experts on a range of important topics—from how to telecommute effectively to how to have more fun in the office
- Reading group materials—including free downloadable discussion guides and an opportunity to obtain free books to get your group started
- A searchable directory of leading experts and speakers, serving as a direct link between you and the experts
- BK's own "Innovative Practices Awards"—links to organizations we believe are helping to lead the way to a more humane workplace

At our recent Berrett-Koehler Community Dialog, BK author Harrison Owen *(Open Space Technology, Expanding Our Now,* and *The Spirit of Leadership)* commented that "the best way to build community is to provide space for community to happen." We hope that bkconnection.com will be such a space. We value your feedback, so please visit us today at www.bkconnection.com and let us know what you think.

Using *Advances in Developing Human Resources* as a Text

The size and style of each issue of *Advances* makes it perfect for use as a text for short courses and workshops, and as a supplemental text for graduate and undergraduate courses. I encourage you to consider using *Advances* in your teaching. For example, we are using issues 1 and 2 as supplemental texts at the University of Minnesota. These two monographs introduce our students to important ideas from fourteen HRD scholars.

We are using *Advances* issue #2—"Action Learning: Successful Strategies for Individual, Team, and Organizational Development" edited by Yorks, O'Neil, and Marsick—as a supplementary text in our Personnel Training and Development course. The primary texts are *Analysis for Improving Performance: Tools for Diagnosing and Documenting Workplace Expertise* by Swanson and *Structured On-the-Job Training: Unleashing Employee Expertise in the Workplace* by Jacobs and Jones.

For our Strategic Planning in HRD course, we are using *Advances* issue #1—"Performance Improvement Theory and Practice" edited by Torraco—as a supplementary text. The primary text is *Improving Performance: Managing the White Space in Organizations* by Rummler and Brache, along with other readings on strategy, scenario building, systems thinking, and quality.

Anyone interested in the syllabi for these two courses should send me an e-mail at swanson2@cris.com. I would also like to hear from you how you are using the *Advances* monographs.

Richard A. Swanson
Editor-in-Chief

Advances in Developing Human Resources

ADVANCES in Developing Human Resources (Advances) is a new and unique kind of HRD publication—a quarterly series of paperbacks, each one focused on a single important topic such as performance improvement, action learning, on-the-job training, intellectual capital, globalization, downsizing, and diversity.

These monographs are edited by, and feature contributions from, some of the top minds in HRD today. Each contributor brings his or her particular expertise to bear on one aspect of the volume's topic.

So each volume in the series is like a seminar in print. You don't just get one person's perspective on one aspect of a topic—you get a complete picture of state-of-the-art thought and practice in a critical area of HRD.

ADVANCES will be an invaluable tool in helping you to develop HRD policies and practices that are rooted in the most forward-looking HRD thinking.

Performance Improvement Theory and Practice
(Advances 1)
Richard Torraco, Editor

1. Theoretical Foundations of Performance Improvement and Implications for Practice, *Richard A. Swanson* 2. Performance Domains and Their Boundaries, *Elwood F. Holton III* 3. Measuring Performance Improvement, *Reid A. Bates* 4. Research Methods for Advancing Performance Improvement, *Darlene Russ-Eft* 5. Case Studies in Performance Improvement, *Martin Mulder* 6. Advancing our Understanding of Performance Improvement, *Richard J. Torraco* 124 pages (March 1999) ISBN 1-58376-011-3

Action Learning: Successful Strategies for Individual, Team, and Organizational Development
(Advances 2)
Lyle Yorks, Judy O'Neil, & Victoria J. Marsick, Editors

1. Action Learning: Theoretical Bases and Varieties of Practice, *Lyle Yorks, Judy O'Neil, Victoria Marsick* 2. Issues in the Design and Implementation of an Action Learning Initiative, *Judy O'Neil, Robert L. Dilworth* 3. Facilitating Action

Learning: The Role of the Learning Coach, *Judy O'Neil* 4. Action Learning for Personal and Transformational Learning, *Robert L. Dilworth, Verna J. Willis* 5. Transfer of Learning from Action Learning Programs to the Organizational Setting, *Lyle Yorks, Sharon Lamm, Judy O'Neil* 6. Organizational Culture Change Through Action Learning, *Glenn Nilson* 7. Action Learning Lessons for Management Development and Organizational Learning, *Lyle Yorks, Judy O'Neil, Victoria Marsick* 8. Annotated Bibliography, *Mary Ragno* 124 pages (June 1999) ISBN: 1-58376-022-9

Informal Learning on the Job
(Advances 3)
Victoria J. Marsick & Marie Volpe, Editors

1. The Nature of and Need for Informal Learning, *Marie Volpe, Victoria J. Marsick* 2. Learning Informally in the Aftermath of Downsizing, *Marie Volpe* 3. Learning Partnerships, *Barbara Keelor (Larson) Lovin* 4. Learning to Be an Effective Team Member, *Sally Vernon* 5. How Managers Learn in the Knowledge Era, *Kathleen Dechant* 6. "Awakening": Developing Learning Capacity in a Small Family Business, *Mary Ziegler* 7. Critical Reflection as a Response to Organizational Disruption, *Ann K. Brooks* 8. Theory and Practice of Informal Learning in the Knowledge Era, *Victoria J. Marsick, Marie Volpe, Karen E. Watkins* 124 pages (September 1999) ISBN 1-58376-023-7

Developing Human Resources in the Global Economy
(Advances 4)
Michael J. Marquardt, Editor

1. Revitalizing HRD for the New Global Millennium, *Mary McAleese* 2. Preparing Human Resources for the Global Economy, *Michael J. Marquardt, Francesco Sofo* 3. Developing Leaders for a Global Consumer Products Company, *Jill Conner, Michael J. Marquardt* 4. Human Resource Issues in Russia: A Case Study, *Nancy O. Berger* 5. The Impact of Globalization on Managerial Learning: The Case of Romania, *Maria Cseh* 6. Individual and Organizational Learning of Chinese Executives at Compaq-China, *Wong Wee Chwee* 7. The Challenges of Globalization and the HRD Response, *Annette Hartenstein* 124 pages (December 1999) ISBN 1-58376-024-5

ORDER FORM

For fastest service, order online through our secure server at bkconnection.com
Call toll-free 7 AM to 12 Midnight: 800-929-2929   Fax to 802-864-7626
Or mail to Berrett-Koeher Communications, PO Box 565, Williston, VT 05495

Subscription to Advances in Developing Human Resources (Item no. 34223-611)

[ ] Individual- $79   [ ] Institutional- $125

For subscription orders outside the United States, please add $15 for surface mail or $30 for air mail.

Single issues: $19.95 each

____ #1, Performance Improvement: Theory and Practice (item no. 60113-611)
____ #2, Action Learning: Successful Strategies for Individual, Team, and Organizational Development (item no. 60229-611)
____ #3, Informal Learning on the Job (item no. 60237-611)
____ #4, Developing Human Resources in the Global Economy (item no. 60245-611)

Quantity discounts on purchases of 10 or more copies of a single title are available. Call Berrett-Koehler Special Sales for more information at 415-288-0260

$ _____ Subtotal
$ _____ Shipping and Handling ($4.50 for one issue, $1.50 for each additional issue)
$ _____ In CA add sales tax
$ _____ Total (Note: No shipping and handling or sales tax on subscriptions.)

Method of Payment

[ ] Payment Enclosed
[ ] Bill me (purchase order number required)   P.O. number _____
[ ] VISA   [ ] MasterCard   [ ] American Express

Card No. _____   Exp. Date _____

Signature _____

Name _____   Title _____

Address _____

City, State, Zip _____

Bill to (if different from Ship to): _____

Name _____   Title _____

Address _____

City, State, Zip _____

Be the first to hear about new publications, special discount offers, exclusive articles, and more! Join the Berrett-Koehler e-mail list!

Your e-mail address _____

Campaign code = 611

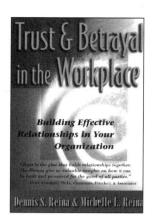

Trust and Betrayal in the Workplace

Building Effective Relationships in
Your Organization
Dennis S. Reina and Michelle L. Reina

- Presents a powerful new research-based model for building trust and healing individuals, teams, and organizations from betrayal
- The first book to identify and define the three kinds of Transactional Trust in a practical framework that can be easily applied to workplace relationships
- Provides Ideas in Action exercises, tips, and real-life examples that illustrate trust-building principles and practices at work

Hardcover, 188 pages
November 1999
ISBN 1-57675-070-1
Item no. 50701-602
$27.95

Trust in the workplace is more important than ever. If organizations are going to survive in the new global economy, their employees must trust themselves and their leaders enough to be willing to take the risks necessary to adapt to the rapidly changing conditions of the marketplace. But after two decades of downsizing, restructuring, and managerial changes, trust within American organizations has reached an all-time low. How can leaders reverse the damage?

Trust and Betrayal in the Workplace provides proven steps to help leaders, employees, and their organizations acknowledge betrayal, solidly recover from it, and rebuild trust. Through in-depth, practical guidelines it clearly explains the dynamics of trust and helps organization members develop a common language to discuss trust-related issues, to identify behaviors that build trust and behaviors that break trust, and to take action on trust-related issues. It provides suggestions, behaviors, and exercises that can be put to use immediately to begin building effective work relationships, productive work environments, and healthy bottom lines.

Trust and Betrayal in the Workplace tells readers everything they need to know about trust: the power unleashed when it exists, the problems created when it doesn't, and the pain suffered when it is betrayed. Through a powerful model that has been successfully applied in organizations in a wide variety of industries, it shows leaders at all levels how to begin the process of healing from betrayal and build an environment that supports trust within themselves, their employees, and their organizations.

Berrett-Koehler
San Francisco

To order call toll-free: **(800) 929-2929**
Internet: www.bkpub.com   Fax: 802-864-7627   Or mail to
Berrett-Koehler Publishers, P.O. Box 565, Williston VT 05495

The Change Handbook

Group Methods for Shaping the Future

Peggy Holman and Tom Devane, Editors

The Change Handbook presents 18 proven change methods together in a single volume. Each method is described in a separate chapter, written by its creator or an expert practitioner. The authors lay out the distinctive aspects of each method, including a story that illustrates its use; answers to frequently asked questions; tips for getting started; an outline of roles, responsibilities, and relationships; impact on power and authority; conditions for success; theory or research base; and keys to sustaining results. The book also includes a comparative matrix that readers can use as a quick reference for understanding the distinctions among methods.

Part 1: Navigating Through Change Methods

Part II: The Methods: Planning

Search Conference, *Merrelyn Emrey and Tom Devane*

Future Search: Acting on Common Ground in Organizations and Communities, *Marvin R. Weisbord and Sandra Janoff*

Method Matters: The Technology of Participation's Participatory Strategic Planning Process, *Marilyn Oyler and John Burbidge*

Strategic Forum, *Chris Soderquist*

The Methods: Structuring

Participative Design Workshop, *Merrelyn Emery and Tom Devane*

Gemba Kaizen: Organizational Change in Real Time, *Masaaki Imai and Brian Haymans*

Fast-Cycle Full-Participation Organizational Redesign, *Alan Scott Fitz and Gary Frank*

Whole Systems Approach, *Cindy Adams and W. A. (Bill) Adams*

The Methods: Adaptable

Preferred Futuring: The Power to Change Whole Systems of Any Size, *Lawrence L. Lippitt*

SimuReal, *Alan Klein and Donald C. Klein*

Organization Workshop, *Barry Oshry*

Whole-Scale Change, *Kathleen D. Dannemiller, Sylvia L. James, and Paul D. Tolchinsky*

Dialogue, *Glenna Gerard and Linda Ellinor*

Open Space Technology, *Harrison Owen (with Anne Stadler)*

Appreciative Inquiry: A Positive Revolution in Change, *David L. Cooperrider and Diana Whitney*

The Conference Model, *Emily and Dick Axelrod*

Think Like a Genius, *Todd Siler*

Real Time Strategic Change, *Robert W. Jacobs and Frank McKeown*

Part III: Closing Thoughts from the Editors

Part IV: Comparative Matrix

Part V: References: Where to Go for More Information

Paperback original, 394 pages
July 1999
ISBN 1-57675-058-2
Item no. 50852-602
$49.95

To order call toll-free: **(800) 929-2929**

Internet: www.bkpub.com   Fax: 802-864-7627   Or mail to

Berrett-Koehler Publishers, P.O. Box 565, Williston VT 05495

Berrett-Koehler
San Francisco